Thornham

A Photographic History of a Norfolk Village and its People

Photographs collected by Pat Thompson.
Researched and written by Peter Oliver.
Produced by John Warham.

This book is affectionately dedicated to the families of *old* Thornham. They have witnessed such huge changes in the village over the last fifty years. It is their photographs and memories which link to tell Thornham's story.

Text copyright Peter Oliver 2006

First published in 2006 by

Thornham Local History Society
Red Brick House
Hall Lane
Thornham PE36 6NB

The right of Peter Oliver to be identified as the author of this work has been asserted in accordance with the Copyright, Designs and Patents Act 1988.

ISBN 978-0-9553333-0-9 / 0-9553333-0-X

A catalogue record for this book is available from the British Library.

Designed by Dick Malt.

Printed by Witley Press, Hunstanton.

Thornham Harbour

The *Jessie Mary*, Thornham's
19th-century trading ship,
operated by Nathaniel
Woods. The 100 ton, two-
master was laid up after her
last voyage in 1914. One
newspaper report suggests
she ended her days as a
Heacham house boat.

The *Jessie Mary* in harbour

The *Jessie Mary* berthed at the Coal Barn, with the Granary in the background.

THORNHAM.

The *Jessie Mary*, berthed at the Coal Barn with Thornham in the background

The way they were. (l-r) The sluice, Granary, Coal Barn and mill.

The Granary

Left: The Coal Barn was once a longer building. The barn came into use with the development of the harbour in the 19th century.

Sailing into Thornham Harbour 1920s style.

John Woods, a Thornham shell-fisherman and owner of the *Abby Onar*. He's thought to have been the father (or possibly uncle) of Nathaniel Woods, master of the *Jessie Mary*. If correct, then John was born in the early 1830s. At the time of the 1901 census, he was aged 68, married to Eleanor and lived in one of the cottages on the south side of The Green.

Thornham's 1843 tithe map shows that members of the Woods and Corston families dominated this area around The Green. The Woods were tenants of two houses, lands and gardens here. The 1841 census lists a grand old lady of the family, 72 year-old Ann Woods, born in the village in 1766. It is believed that mariner Nat Woods lived in Bay Tree Cottage in the High Street from 1914 to his death in 1936.

Today, one of the last links with the old Woods family is Eric Beck. He married the late Rene Woods, whose father was Jack Woods, a nephew of 19th-century sailor Nat.

Top: George Hogge originally built two granaries. One was demolished in the early 20th century. The second Granary, above, was hit by a couple of 'friendly' shells during the Second World War, and suffered more damage afterwards when a mine was detonated nearby. There was flood damage to the building in 1953 and eventually it was demolished.

The upper floor of the Granary was used as an artists' studio. Before the Second World War, families spent their summer holidays there.

The Coal Barn 'disguised' as Pip's house for BBC Television's adaptation of Charles Dickens' *Great Expectations* in 1998.

It took several men to shut down the sluice at the top of the tide. At low tide, the sluice was raised and the following rush of water helped to keep the channel clear for shipping. This photograph shows the sluice after maintenance work in 1913. Nearly 60 years later, Tim Siddle renovated the whole structure again.

Nearly fifty years ago, writer Eric Fowler, otherwise known to readers of the *Eastern Daily Press* as *Jonathan Mardle*, visited Thornham, once the home port of the *Jessie Mary*, and struck up a conversation with an old gentleman he met on The Green. In the following article about the economy of 19th-century East Coast harbours, Eric wrote:

My gentleman, 80 years of age, had lived in his youth through the last days of the old economy. He used to work as a lad at Thornham Mill, where he had learnt what is now the almost lost art of dressing the mill stones. That is cutting fresh grooves in the stones when they had got worn down. It was done with a special tool, which is now so rare, called a mill bill … he pointed westward across the marsh to a lonely brick building. 'The Granaries are near there,' he said. 'And that's the Coal Barn. It was where we used to unload the coal. It belonged to Nat Woods. He bought a 120-ton ship to fetch coal from Lynn. Then he found she wasn't big enough. So he got her up on to the hard on a very high tide and cut her in half and put another twelve feet into her. And he re-stepped the mast too.'

Thornham's Ted Rason saw the *Jessie Mary* come into harbour as a young boy.

He recalled: *'When I was about seven, I was told of the ship bringing in a load of coal. I was excited and it was on a Saturday so off I go … when I got to the harbour the ship wasn't there as the tide was not in. I had to wait half an hour for the ship to arrive and then the unloading began. The two men, Nat Woods, the owner, and Jack Potter, the helper, put two planks from the ship to the home-made bridge and started to carry the coal off in bushel skeps (56lb baskets). Darned hard work. They had a horse and wagon to deliver the coal around the village. Nat Woods lived opposite the Chequers Inn. (Bay Tree Cottage) and Jack Potter lived at Primrose Cottage with his parents and sister.'*

In 1866 several fishing boats were operating from Thornham and in 1901 there were still four shell-fishermen working out of the harbour.

The Village Mill

Thornham Mill. A notice in the field beside the mill used to warn: *Admission to this field is free. The Bull will charge later.*

A model of the mill, made by Kenneth Hamlin of Heacham, is displayed in the parish church

In the church there are some
cleverly crafted figures on the
pew ends. This one shows an
old windmill. Others portray the
sins of drunkenness, anger and
laziness.

With the summer harvest safely gathered in, the women and girls of 19th century Thornham gleaned the fields, gathering up any ears of corn left behind. They would thresh the ears themselves and then take the corn to the village miller to be ground into baking flour. Nothing went to waste in the old days.

The Crane family were flour millers in Thornham for at least three or more generations in the 18th and early 19th centuries.

Faden's 18th-century map pinpoints an early Thornham mill near Long Wood (off the New or Ringstead Road). Bryant's map of 1826 shows two mills, the harbour mill and a second one by the old chalk pit on New Road .

The evidence suggests that the Long Wood mill was moved to the harbour in the 1880s, but it is impossible today to say for sure.

Howes Tipple, a member of an old village family, was the last working miller in Thornham. He was listed in 1896 as working for Elizabeth Crane, the last mill owner. Two years later the mill was up for sale. Thornham's mill had ground itself to a standstill.

The skeleton mill was finally blown down in a gale in 1928. Some of the working parts of the mill are stored at Gressenhall Rural Life Museum.

Smuggling Days

Coastguard Cottages with the
pond known as *Monty's Pit*,
named after Monty Bell who
lived close by.

3212. THE GREEN & COASTGUARD STATION, THORNHAM.

Oswald Waterfield, landlord at the Lifeboat Inn for many years, used to tell an old smuggling story related to him by his mother, Alice, who died in 1946.

It told of an ageing 19th-century Thornham man, who had been involved in smuggling tobacco. Alice said that the man's loft was often piled high with tobacco, and told how he regularly took his booty to Wisbech in a horse-drawn cart.

Violet Ames, a member of the family who lived in Thornham in the early years of the 20th century, appears to have heard a similar story. In her notes on the History of Thornham, she writes of a Thornham man who

…went out to sea on the pretext of fetching coals, but by a strange coincidence on every return journey he always ran aground before safely reaching port … his cargo had to be lightened by horses and carts making their way over the marshes in the dead of night. It is also strange that the same men's carts always helped him …

Smuggling had been part of Thornham's local economy for many a year. Heavily taxed gin, tea and tobacco were the main goods involved. Remote beaches were used as 'dropping off' points.

In Thornham in 1782, Wells Excise men were attacked by a gang of smugglers 'armed with firearms, pokers and pitchforks'. Apparently the smugglers had just recovered 26lbs of tea which had earlier been uncovered by the Customs men. The head officer was crippled by six blows to the head in the incident.

A year later the Excise men dug up 4 cwt of tea buried in the sand at Thornham, and, in 1783, a local farmer and two smugglers were arrested and whisked away to London to be tried. Local juries rarely found smugglers guilty. Locals, sometimes the vicar or squire, had a vested interest.

Just forty years later, smuggled tobacco would have been on the mind of Thornham coastguard Mark Butcher. Tobacco smuggling was still big business on this part of the coast well into the 20th century. Mark was an early member of a family who would, over the next 175 years, bring together the local family names of Matthews, Parnell, Hughes, Nudds and Langford.

Links to 19th-century man, Mark Butcher, continue to grow. Current village resident Neville Nudds is his great grandson, and Jenny (née Smith) Langford, a great great great granddaughter.

Tales of smugglers' tunnels are the stuff of Thornham legend. Perhaps the the best known is a suspected tunnel leading from Stocks Hill House, opposite the Methodist Chapel, to the old Chequers Inn. Certainly, the large cellar and alcoves beneath the house wouldn't rule that out.

Barry and Jenny Langford

Smuggling territory –
Coastguard Cottages on
the right, with two of the
three Second World War
observation/triangulation
towers in the background.
The left-hand one stands
on Dutchwoman's Hill.

Love, the *Lydia* and the Lifeboat Inn

An 1890s photograph showing onlookers watching horses launch the Brancaster lifeboat from the beach. This is how, and from where, the *Lily Bird* would have been launched in 1881.

Below: Vincent Sadler, local baker, uncle to Olive Waterfield, in 1915.

The sailing ship *Lydia* aground near Thornham in 1881.

Early on the morning of October 23rd, 1881, fishermen at Wells spotted the Norwegian barque *Lydia* close to shore and running before a violent easterly gale. Fisherman John Harman, who witnessed the incident, recalled a friend beside him saying: 'If she doesn't alter course, she'll be aground.'

Very soon afterwards, the ship foundered close to the Thornham shore. The Brancaster lifeboat, *Lily Bird* was launched from the old lifeboat site at Brancaster golf clubhouse at 9 a.m, and the crew found the *Lydia* already missing its main topmast, its rudder badly damaged and water flooding the hold. The fourteen-strong crew were picked up, taken ashore and delivered to the Ship Inn at Brancaster to be looked after.

Their arrival at the pub would have caused a great stir in the village. Perhaps young Vincent Sadler, who became a Brancaster baker, popped in to see the new arrivals. His parents ran the Lifeboat Inn in Thornham. It was also home to Vincent's sister, Mary Ann.

We'll never know what happened exactly, but Helmer Petersen, one of the crew from the *Lydia*, met, fell in love with and married Mary Ann. They made their home in the village. Their children included Frank Sadler Petersen, Vincent Helmer Petersen and Eva.

The crew of the *Lydia* thanked local people in a note published in a King's Lynn newspaper:

The crew return their sincere thanks to Mr. H. Jarvis, landlord of the Ship Inn for the kindness which he displayed towards them…much credit is also due to Mr. Pointer for so quickly providing eight powerful horses to launch the lifeboat…

Local lifeboat folklore tells how, when a maroon was fired to alert the crew in the days of horse-launched lifeboats, the animals recognised the signal and were always excited and ready for work. They liked nothing better than a salty bath as they towed the lifeboat into deeper water.

The Village School

Copper Hall (just beyond the horse chestnut tree) was a pre-1850s school room.

4373- The Street, Thornham

The Old School Room (or Reading Room), beside the former King's Head, was used as a classroom in the old days and became a regular meeting place for Parish Council meetings. Early in the Second World War, George Wilson, landlord at the King's Head, made it Home Guard HQ. In later years it was also used for cookery classes.

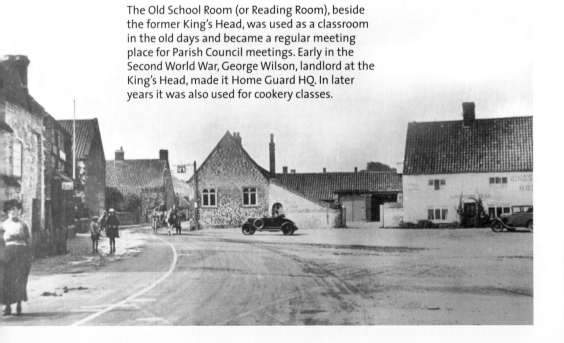

Above: Some 19th and turn-of-the-20th-century pupils at Thornham School.

Thornham schoolchildren playing in the High Street.

William Hogge built the new Thornham School in 1854. The school finally closed in 1985 when the County Education Authority decided there were not enough village children to make it sustainable. A group of local people climbed the clock tower and 'kidnapped' the school bell in protest at the closure. Nearly 20 years later, it was returned and presented to the new owners of the building in return for a donation to the church.

More Thornham School pupils.

The Iron Lady ... Edith Ames Lyde

Edith Eliza, daughter of William Samuel Hogge
(later Mrs. Ames Lyde), as a young woman.

Mrs. Edith Ames Lyde (1850-1914), Thornham's Lady of the Manor (left), outside The Red House with Mrs. Evelyn Grange, who was Eileen Richmond's mother. The Grange Family lived in the house in the years before the First World War.

Right: Mrs. Ames Lyde out sailing in Thornham harbour.

Thornham's Red Cross nurses
ready for inspection.

Right: Two of Thornham's Red
Cross nurses, Posy and Barbara
Villiers.

Opposite: Queen Alexandra,
Edith Ames Lyde and Victor
Ames at The Cottage for the
royal inspection of Thornham's
British Red Cross nurses in 1911,
and a display of first aid
techniques.

In November 1881, Edith Ames Lyde, Lady of the Manor of Thornham, and her husband Lionel, journeyed to Sandringham to attend the Prince and Princess of Wales' County Ball, a glittering occasion attended by the cream of Norfolk society.

In the years ahead, Edith would surprise Norfolk society by becoming a business woman; a rare pursuit for women of her class and social position. The company she founded was Ames-Lyde, Elsum and Co, better known as Thornham Ironworks (see next article). She was also a noted local politician.

Christened Edith Eliza Hogge, she was a direct descendant of George Hogge, the King's Lynn merchant who built Thornham Hall and The Red House in the 18th century.

In 1873, she married Captain Lionel Ames, of the Grenadier Guards. He added the 'Lyde' tag, a 'taken' or inherited family name, to their marriage title. But it does seem that, although he used a hyphen in the name, Edith's signature shows she didn't; some social nuance there perhaps. When Edith appeared in the streets of Thornham, it's said she would be met with an immediate doffing of men's caps and bobbing women.

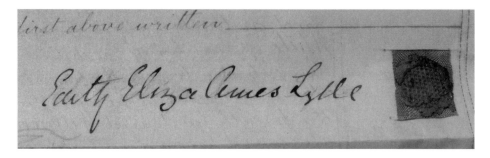

Lionel died in 1883 and his widow, heartbroken, so they say, took to her widow's weeds, and spent the rest of her life pursuing good works in the village.

Edith was the power behind the celebrated Thornham and Titchwell Horticultural Show, and she also founded the local branches of the Red Cross Society, the Territorial Force (the precursor of the Territorial Army) and Scouts and Guides. She was also a member of the Parish Council and President of Thornham Cricket Club, whose home ground was in the Park behind her home.

Violet (née Napier) Ames with her camera on
Thornham beach in 1913. Several of the
photographs in this book, covering the period
1910 to 1930, were taken by her. She and husband
Victor Ames built Marshlands. Their children, Joan
and Maurice, the last Ames to live in Thornham,
are still fondly remembered by many villagers.
Victor's brother Lionel married Edith Hogge, the
Lady of Thornham Manor, and a third brother,
Oswald, built Thornham's new Manor.

The Ames albums, three volumes of family
photographs, can be seen in the Norwich
Millennium Library.

Left: Iron workers in 1905. The photograph includes co-founder and schoolmaster William Elsum, Walter Potter and Reggie Allen, the boy (centre) with the watch chain. Reggie became office clerk at the works.

Left: Noah Francis (extreme left, front row), grandfather to Eric, Lionel and Kenny, was a talented iron worker. He created a beautiful rose to give to his wife.

Below: Noah and his wife in later years with their rose.

Vic Hardy, a modern day Thornham ironworker

Mrs. Ames Lyde's brother-in-law, Victor Ames (right), working up a design at Thornham ironworks.

A showcase of ironwork in Oak House.

Below: A view of the High Street and the site of the Iron Works (on the left), which closed in 1916. Lennie Plume, who had worked at the ironworks, opened a blacksmith and wheelwright's shop here soon after. Lennie's daughter, Rene Hunt says: 'When I was very young I remember tumbrels and wagons turning up to have their wheels repaired. Red hot iron tyres were put on the wheels. Then my father and mother, both with sledge hammers, would knock the rims on. It was hard work.'

Prior to their departure from Sandringham for Windsor, the King and Queen, accompanied by Princess Victoria, Prince Philip of Saxe-Coburg, and several ladies and gentlemen, motored over to Thornham and paid a visit of inspection to the ironworks that have been established there

A local newspaper report of the 1905 visit to Thornham by King Edward VII and Queen Alexandra

Edith Ames Lyde's initial idea for the ironworks had been to create an evening pastime for villagers. But the business took off and Edith formed the company, Ames Lyde, Elsum and Co to market the ironwork at home and around the world.

One of her brothers-in-law, Victor Ames, joined the business as a designer. Among the firm's customers were Queen Victoria, King Edward VII and Queen Alexandra, the Spencers of Althorp House, and Lady Rothschild of Tring Park. The latter's orders included lamp fittings, bronzed and silver-bronzed caskets and a set of graveyard gates.

Edith was in India at the time of the famous royal visit to the ironworks so the day was hosted by her other brother-in-law, Major Oswald Ames, of Thornham Manor. At 6' 8" tall he had been the tallest man in the British Army, and was also the officer who led 50,000 troops through London in 1897 as part of Queen

Victoria's Diamond Jubilee celebrations. He built this portrait of the Queen into a wall at The Manor.

The purpose of the royal visit was to inspect garden gates being made for Sandringham. During the visit, the Queen observed: 'I must have a hand in making one of our gates' and, with that, she was allowed to take a hammer and shape a piece of metal.

Mrs. Ames Lyde at work in the ironworks.

Street Scenes

The road from Church Street to The Green was once just a dirt track.

High Street. Over the years some buildings have vanished – some were condemned by early slum clearance legislation in the late 30s and 40s.

Above: Looking towards Malthouse Farm barns (distant right) with Jones' (or Old) Farm on the left. Daphne Sadler, who married builder Tim Siddle, was born in Jones' Farm. The pond, known as Jones' Pit, is still there today, hidden beneath years of debris.

Main Road looking east.

The School Room (Reading Room) beside the King's Head. The buildings attached to the School Room included two cottages, one of which was home to Shirley Riseborough, who later married John Lake. Shirley's parents were Marshall and Dorothy Riseborough. On Shirley's birthday in December 1945, an army lorry skidded on ice at the King's Head corner and smashed into the cottage. Fortunately, Shirley was at school and her mother at work. The damage was extensive and the family moved out. Mrs. Monk lived in the second cottage.

Old maps show that Hall Lane was also known as Hall Reach or Winter's Lane.

The above photograph is one of six in this book taken by Herbert Coates of Wisbech and reproduced by courtesy of the copyright holders, the Wisbech and Fenland Museum. Herbert Coates had a portrait studio in Wisbech, but later made a living by travelling, particularly on the East Coast and Derbyshire, photographing local village street scenes and selling his postcards through local stores. His business ran through to the 1960s. A large collection of his photographs and negatives, some 8000 in all, were found slowly deteriorating in a garage by a Wisbech antique dealer who donated them to the museum.

The white-painted building end-on to the High Street, between the barn and Valentine Cottage, was where blacksmith Jim Tipple had his forge. Jim later lived at No 1 Green Lane. The Tipples were a large village family. Jim's cousin was Howes Tipple, Thornham's last miller. Jim himself was uncle to Eva and Adie.

This High Street barn was used to store coal in the early 20th century. The woman pushing the wheelbarrow is believed to be Mrs. Esther Siddle, mother of Tim and grandmother to Adrian Siddle. In the 1920/30s Frank Callaby ran this business. On summer weekends he cleaned up the family coal lorry and transported Thornham cricketers to away matches.

Entering the village from Holme.

Thornham – a hundred years ago

The 1901 census showed that there were 627 people living in Thornham, 302 men and 325 women. That was just about Thornham's lowest population in nearly a hundred years; partly due to industrialisation and an increasing flow of people from village to town and city.

The list of village surnames at the time: Allen, Andrews, Arter, Asker, Auker, Barber, Baring, Barker, Batterbee, Bayfield, Bayliss, Beck, Bell, Bond, Bridges, Britton, Bull, Bunting, Burley, Bush, Bussey, Butters, Callaby, Chestney, Chilvers, Clark, Cobb, Cook, Cooper, Corston, Davis, Diggins, Dix, Dodds, Ducker, Eagle, Elsum, Everitt, Ewen, Fenton, Francis, Frohawk, Gibson, Graham, Grange, Green, Groundsell, Haines, Heading, Helsdon, Herring, Hickman, Hill, Hilling, Hines, Hinson, Hooks, Hooper, Howard, Hubbard, Hughes, Hunt, Jarvis, Johnson, Jones, Kingdow, Knights, Lake, Langley, Lee, Leeder, Lewis, Lord, Manser, Matthews, Mayes, Melton, Mickleburgh, Middleton, Mitchell, Moore, Morris, Neale, Newcombe, Newell, Nudds, Nurse, Pond, Parnell, Patrick, Pearmain, Petersen, Petts, Pike, Pointer, Potter, Powell, Proctor, Proudfoot, Rason, Ratcliffe, Ray, Renaut, Ringwood, Robbins, Roberts, Roper, Rumbellow, Rutland, Sadler, Sallaband, Sampson, Sands, Savage, Seapey, Sellening, Seppings, Shellaly, Siddle, Smith, Smithbone, Softley, Southerland, Sporne, Starling, Sutherland, Taylor, Thacker, Tipple, Tulloch, Wadlow, Wagg, Walden, Walker, Waterfield, Whiting, Williamson, Wilson, Woods, Wright, Wyatt and Yaxley.

The census population breakdown noted 125 pupils attending Thornham School, 60 agricultural and general labourers, 32 servants (including housekeepers and housemaids) and 16 people, including employers, living on their 'own means'.

There were 12 horse teamsters or teamers (the men who looked after the teams of farm horses), 8 shop assistants, 12 metal workers, 6 farmers, 6 stockmen, 6 fishermen, 6 farm yardmen, 5 bricklayers, 5 gardeners, 4 butchers, 4 carpenters, 3 innkeepers, 3 grocers, 3 schoolmistresses, 3 bakers, 3 carters, 2 road menders, 2 drapers, 2 coastguard boatmen, 2 naval pensioners, 2 gamekeepers, 2 dress-makers/tailors, 2 blacksmiths (and 4 helpers), 2 wheelwrights, 2 shepherds and 2 nurses.

There was also a barber, chimney sweep, church clerk, coachman, coal merchant, cook, cow keeper, farm engine driver, golf green keeper, governess, groom, harness maker, laundress, milliner, naval reserve officer, night scavenger (night soil remover), postmaster, postmistress, postal clerk, retired farm bailiff, retired seaman, sailor, schoolmaster, ship's captain, shorthand clerk, straw hat maker, surgeon, vicar, wheelwright and apprentice and woodman.

'Every able-bodied man should know how to use a rifle...'

The Church Magazine of 1907 gives some illuminating comments on life in Thornham as seen by the then vicar, the Rev. Nathan Waller.

The vicar complains: *I hoped that we might have had a better congregation at the 4 o'clock service on Christmas Day …*

Sunday services are now being held at 8am, 11am, 3pm and 6.30pm

The vicar writes: *Avoid as much as you can, Dances, Parties and Entertainments in Lent … practice some form of self denial. Go without something, give up something or make a point of doing something for others …*

Mrs. Ames Lyde has given a present to each child at the annual 'Christmas treat'.

James Groundsell was laid to rest. He had entered the Navy in 1844 and served in the Baltic during the Crimean War. The vicar notes: *His body was born to the grave by the Bluejackets…*

A play entitled 'The Parish Council', and performed by nine lads, had, said the vicar, *created great laughter…*

The vicar writes: *There are in this parish more than 200 adults who never go to church or to chapel and who are leading Heathen lives …*

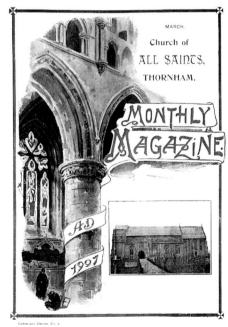

The Rev. Waller with the Church Lads' Brigade rifle squad.

The vicar notes: ...*it is reckoned on the average about 300 people enter the Church on a Sunday. If that is correct and if each gave one penny a Sunday, the collections each Sunday would be £1 5s. The totals (actually) work out at just one halfpenny per head. Is this quite as it should be? The vicar gives two shillings each Sunday.*

The vicar left the village in 1908 to do missionary work in Burma, but continued to contribute to the parish magazine with regular newsletters. Soon after arriving, he writes of a jungle trip. *I saw fresh tracks of 2 leopards and a tiger, but I did not get the opportunity of a shot...*

One of the last magazine notes the vicar wrote before he left was as follows: *Bertie Fenton won first prize in the Church Lads Brigade rifle competition. Bertie fought in the Boer War. The day may come when England will call upon her sons to defend this land we love. Every able-bodied man should know how to use a rifle if necessary. It should be a mark of manhood. There ought only to be two classes in this country. Men who can use a rifle if needed, old women who cannot do so. To which class do we belong?*

Thornham Under Attack

Late one summer night in 1909, members of the Sandringham Company of the newly-formed 5th Battalion (Territorials) Norfolk Regiment launched a midnight exercise 'attack' on their Thornham counterparts.

A few weeks later, King Edward VII presented the regiment's new colours. To celebrate the occasion, the Sandringham Company invited Thornham's territorials to join them on the Royal Estate for some tub-thumping speeches, patriotic songs and recitations.

Captain Frank Beck, the King's land agent and the Sandringham Company's commanding officer, made a speech welcoming the Thornham guests. The local newspaper report read:

In giving the toast to the health of the visitors, he (Frank Beck) *alluded to their sister company, the Thornham men … that gallant little company* (50 or so men at the time) *on the coast. A short time ago the Sandringham Company marched on Thornham at midnight. The result of the conflict that followed was, he understood, that the Sandringham men decimated the enemy, and the enemy decimated the Sandringham men (Laughter). However, after they had been decently buried, they very much enjoyed an excellent breakfast which Mrs. Ames Lyde provided for them … he* (Mr. Beck) *congratulated them on their commander, Lieut. Coxon, who was a veritable steam engine of energy and kindness (applause). He also congratulated the Thornham men on their old war-horse, or as he was known, their shaft-horse, Colour-Sergeant Kendal (Applause).*

The newspaper report showed that it was a most jovial occasion with much banter about which territorials would be hiding in rabbit holes should they ever face a real enemy.

The occasion also heard how the territorials hoped they would soon be qualified to join the regulars in a real fight. A dignitary hoped that if the occasion arose, the men of the 5th Battalion (Territorials) would not *rush into battle and all get killed in a hurry …*

History and the First World War battleground of Gallipoli would prove that remark tragically close to the truth for some of them.

The End of an Era

Victor Ames with a shooting party
and house guests.

Afternoon tea at The Cottage, the home of Edith and Lionel Ames Lyde.

The Ames children, Joan and Maurice (standing), father Victor in the back, with Alfred Cobb at the rear wheel.

Victor Ames outside Ivy Cottage on his way to Church.

Alfred Cobb, gardener at Marshlands, gives a ride in a home-made punt to Joan and Maurice, as their father, Victor, looks on.

CHURCH PAGEANT, THORNHAM 1909

Above: Dancers at a Vicarage Pageant. In a Parish Magazine, the Vicar says that the 1907 Pageant had been designed to: *... set forth the needs of heathen nations. Groups of children representing India, Africa, Japan, China and Greenland, and dressed to suggest those countries, appeal to other children to send help to them. The entrance of the cross, escorted by choirboys and the colours carried and guarded by members of the Church Lads Brigade, are intended to set forth the Church's answer to the appeal of heathen nations who plead for our assistance ...*

Opposite, top: Coronation Day 1910

Centre: Fashions on show during Thornham's Flower Show/Athletics Day.

Bottom: Some of the Thornham Church Lads Brigade gun crew, seen here in 1906, would soon be shooting for real (l-r): H. Edge, Arthur Renaut, Jack Sporne, who was Thornham's vermin killer, Mr. Gretton, the coastguard, Frank Petersen, the son of Helmer, G. Dix, George Mayes, James Asker, a relative of Margaret Bunkle, R. Williamson, W. Hickman, J. Roper, S. Frohawk and J. Walker. The Reverend Nathan Waller paid for the building of Thornham's Drill Hall as a home for the All Saints' Company of the Church Lads Brigade. It is now used as the village hall, a place for dances, meetings and other functions.

Below: Dancing around the vicarage maypole

Edith Ames Lyde was a prime organiser behind the long established annual Thornham and Titchwell Horticultural Show. The way it was run very much reflected the old Victorian class system that was just beginning to break down.

The entry classes were: *Cottagers* for ordinary folk, *Honorary* for the green-fingered upper classes, *Trade* for the working folk and *Children*.

In future, aristocratic autumn-sown onions and shallots would challenge cottage cucumbers and cabbages on equal ground.

Newspaper cuttings show that Edith won many of the events she entered (*Honorary*). Her brother-in-law, Oswald Ames (Thornham Manor), Mrs. Heading (The Hall) and Major The Hon. Gilbert Legh (Drove House) were always among the prize winners too.

In the *Cottager* class of 1905, the most green-fingered Thornham residents included Mrs. S. Bell, broad beans and turnips; H. Hines, carrots; T. Auker, peas; Mrs. Eagle, blackcurrants; Widow Johnson, carnations; S. Proudfoot, rhubarb; May Rason, fuchsias and Mrs. R. Bussey, sweet peas. The *Trade* section starred J. Ducker's red cherries, Mrs. Frank Callaby's cucumbers and Miss Lewis' best eggs.

The same newspaper report also covered the Thornham and Titchwell's Annual Village Sports which took place on the same day.

The village sports produced some good sprinters, and afforded in the 'laced boots' struggle, and other events, amusements for all. … with the exception of one shower, the weather held fair until after dark and happily it was not until 11 at night that the storm, which had been threatening for many days, broke over the ground …an adjournment was afterwards made to The Cottage grounds, where dancing was kept up to the music of the Wells Town Band until a late hour…

Among the top athletes of the day were blacksmith Sam Yaxley and W. Batterbee (the 3-legged and coat and waistcoat races), Mr. Diggins (flat race), Alfred Cobb (mile race), N. Nudds (mile walk) and W. Potter (laced-boots struggle). Mr. Potter also won the 'Comic costume' men's race.

It would be some time before the village would laugh again at men racing in funny costumes.

The year 1913, particularly, seemed to herald the beginnings of another age.

That was the year when blacksmith Sam Yaxley collapsed and died after rolling the cricket square. It was also the year that Thornham's oldest inhabitant, Mrs. Elizabeth Eagle passed away. She was 94 and had left four sons and a daughter, 32 grandchildren and 30 great-grandchilden.

There was one new beginning that year. Victor Ames married Violet Napier, and they would spend much of their married life in Thornham. The bride wore a diamond and platinum pendant that Mrs. Ames Lyde had given her.

But Mrs. Ames Lyde's life was just about over. In March the next year, the Lady of Thornham Manor, who had been an inveterate traveller, died in China. The family fulfilled her request: *Where I die, there let me be buried.*

The report of the memorial service held in Thornham Church noted:

Quiet little knots of grave-looking villagers began to collect near the churchyard gates at an early hour in the afternoon, but the majority remained outside watching the assembling detachments of Territorials, Red Cross units and troops of boy scouts … all the seats inside the church were taken and a large number of people, mainly Thornham villagers, had to content themselves with standing room …

It was the end of an era.

Descended from the same family line as Edith Ames Lyde, Stephen Bett, the current Lord of the Manor, is seen here with his family (l-r) Harry, Claudia, Phillipa and Olivia.

For King and Country

A pre-war photograph of Mrs. Ames Lyde's Thornham Territorials. (Probable l-r) back row, George Mayes, Charlie Bridges, unidentified, ? Woods, Jack Woods, Alfred Cobb (Henry's father); front, blacksmith Jim Tipple (another member of his family, Robert, was also in the Territorials), Jacob Walker (he's got the stripe) and Alfred Greef (Henry's father). Alfred always thought he made a lucky move when, just before war broke out, he left the Thornham Territorials and joined the Norfolk Regulars. By 1915 Thornham's Territorials were fighting in a nightmare called Gallipoli. Alfred didn't escape though. He was wounded on the Western Front.

Off to war. Albert Walker, brother of Jacob and father of Luan (Llewellyn) and Vera.

Another photograph of Thornham
Territorials, who left Thornham on
the day after war was declared.

Just two Thornham boys who went
to war ... Henry (H.G.) Proudfoot and
Sam Proudfoot (S.E.). They both died.

Oswald Ames	Herbert Mitchell
Charles Bridges,	Ambrose Mitchell
William Bull,	William Matsell
Francis B. Bett	Albert G. Mann
Stafford H. I. Bett	Charles Middleton
Arthur E. Back	Robert Nudds
Arthur Bell	Fredrick W. Proudfoot
Thomas Bussey	Sam Proudfoot
Alfred Cobb	Harry Proudfoot
Nathaniel Corston	Percy Proudfoot
Thomas Dix	Philip Parnell
Peter Dix	John Potter
William Ducker	Frank Petersen
James Ducker	Ambrose Rason
Wilfred Dunston	Tom Rason
Frank Fenton	Murrell Roper
Bertie Fenton	James Roper
Stephen B. Fenton	Tom Rumbellow
Ernest Fenton	Victor Rumbellow
Samuel Francis	Alfred Siddle
William Groundsell	Samuel Siddle
Alfred Greef	Robert Siddle
Walter Gent	William Siddle
Clifford Grange	Walter Siddle
Neville Helsdon	Thomas Siddle
Victor Helsdon	William Smith
Thomas Haines	Stephen Smith
George Alec Heading	Amos Sutherland
Richard T. Heading	Charles Thacker
Robert B. Heading	Robert Tipple
Stephen Hewitt	Edward Thompson
Horace Hewitt	Jack Villiers
Edward Herring	Albert Walker
David Hilling	Charles Williamson
Charles Hines	Robert Williamson
Reuben Hickman	Charles Woods
Leonard R. Lewis	John Woods
Peter Legh	Henry Wyatt
John Lake	William Wright

WILLIAM N.I. ASKER
CHARLES BAKER
GEORGE ALBERT BELL
THOMAS BELL
FREDERICK JOHN BEVAN
ROBERT CHESTNEY
JOHN BRAVEN DYER
ROBERT FRANCIS
SIDNEY FROHAWK
HARRY FRANK HICKMAN
FREDERICK E. HICKMAN
GEORGE W. JOHNSON
WILLIAM PARNELL
SAMUEL W. SMITHBONE

The list of Thornham soldiers who went to war.

Left: Thornham sailors who went to war.

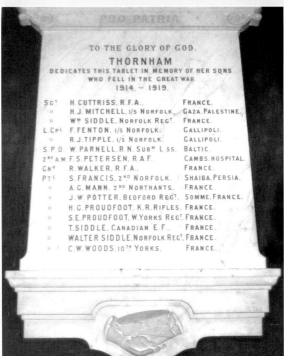

PRO PATRIA

TO THE GLORY OF GOD.

THORNHAM

DEDICATES THIS TABLET IN MEMORY OF HER SONS
WHO FELL IN THE GREAT WAR
1914 – 1919.

Sgt	H. CUTTRISS, R.F.A.,	FRANCE.
"	H. J. MITCHELL, 1/5 NORFOLK,	GAZA, PALESTINE.
"	Wm SIDDLE, NORFOLK REGt.	FRANCE.
L.Cpl	F. FENTON, 1/5 NORFOLK.	GALLIPOLI.
"	R. J. TIPPLE, 1/5 NORFOLK.	GALLIPOLI.
S.P.O.	W. PARNELL, R.N. SUBm L 55.	BALTIC.
2ND A.M	F. S. PETERSEN, R.A.F.	CAMBS. HOSPITAL.
Gnr	R. WALKER, R.F.A.	FRANCE.
Pte	S. FRANCIS, 2nd NORFOLK.	SHAIBA, PERSIA.
"	A. G. MANN, 2nd NORTHANTS.	FRANCE.
"	J. W. POTTER, BEDFORD REGt.	SOMME, FRANCE.
"	H. G. PROUDFOOT, K. R. RIFLES.	FRANCE.
"	S. E. PROUDFOOT, W. YORKS REGt.	FRANCE.
"	T. SIDDLE, CANADIAN E.F.	FRANCE.
"	WALTER SIDDLE, NORFOLK REGt.	FRANCE.
"	C. W. WOODS, 10th YORKS.	FRANCE.

Above: Local Red Cross staff and patients outside Thornham's Red House, which became a convalescent hospital with 25 beds. Doris Smith's Aunt Agnes (Bell) was a nurse there at the time. She met Joe Wright, a wounded Canadian soldier, in the hospital. They married and settled in Canada.

The church memorial lists the sixteen Thornham men who made the ultimate sacrifice.

Right: Frank Sadler Petersen, a son of Helmer (a crewman on the *Lydia*), died during war service.

ON WAR SERVICE

A Souvenir of the
GREAT EUROPEAN WAR 1914/15

THE DAILY MIRROR, Saturday, September 8, 1928.

LOOK OUT FOR FRASS ON HIS NEW TOUR NEXT WEEK

Daily Mirror

THE DAILY PICTURE PAPER WITH THE LARGEST NET SALE

No. 7,744   Registered at the G.P.O. as a Newspaper   SATURDAY, SEPT. 8, 1928   One Penny

L 55's FORTY TWO DEAD BURIED IN ONE GRAVE

The coffins of the forty-two members of the crew of the British submarine L 55, sunk in the Baltic in 1919 and recently raised, being placed side by side in one large grave at the Royal Naval Cemetery at Haslar, Portsmouth, yesterday. Flowers sent from all parts of the world were carried in the mile-long procession, and clergy of all denominations took part in the graveside service. Naval bands played funeral marches and a party of bluejackets fired volleys. See also page 32.—(Daily Mirror photograph.)

The *Daily Mirror* front page covers the burial of the crew from submarine L55, including Thornham's William Parnell.

In July, 1914, Thornham Cricket Club beat Snettisham by over 200 runs to become Sandringham League champions. The next fixture for several of the Thornham team would be, in the language of the time, against 'the Hun'.

That 1914 team consisted of T. Bussey, R.B. Heading, F. Woolerton, R.T. Heading, teacher E.Y. Thompson, the Rev. F.C. Moore, W. Gent, S. Renaut, G. Lee, T. Renaut. and George Heading. At least six members of the Thornham Cricket Club served in the First World War.

The Thornham Bowls team also played a last pre-war game on the green behind the Chequers pub. The village team included: W.R. Johnson, T.E. Sutherland, J.W. Ducker, Lewis Mitchell, Alfred Greef, J. Meek, R.W. Johnson and B. E. Watson. Four of them are recorded as going to war.

On August 5, the day after war was declared, the 11.30 am Hunstanton–King's Lynn train was full of soldiers, including the late Mrs. Edith Ames Lyde's Thornham men of the 1/5th Battalion, Norfolk Regiment(Territorial Force).

At King's Lynn station the local newspaper reporters saw the Thornham men change trains and join other units on the 12.30 a.m. train for East Dereham (battalion HQ).

The Lynn Company was joined by the Downham, Hunstanton and Thornham detachments, and the Gatling guns of the Battalion, on the same train. The men spent the time in waiting for the departure of the train in singing patriotic and other popular songs, 'Rule Britannia' being a special favourite … the train started its journey at 18 minutes to one, being delayed on account of the lateness of the London train, and as it commenced to leave, the Mayor called for three cheers for the King. The Territorials came to the salute, all male civilians baring their heads … the train however only drew out of the station and then returned to pick up some other carriages. As it did so, the Territorials were heartily cheered, and, as they left, they in turn gave the Mayor three hearty cheers. On the line the railway men had placed a number of fog signals and these went off with deafening effect. It was a real railwayman's 'God Speed.'

A Norfolk, and Thornham, Tragedy

For Thornham working men such as Robert James Tipple, Frank Fenton, Herbert James Mitchell, Neville Helsdon and other village young men, the idea of a cruise aboard the *Aquitania*, one of the most luxurious ships of the age, might have proved attractive at any other time.

But the year was 1915, the ship was overcrowded with troops and its destination was Gallipoli.

On July 29th, Thornham's territorials, who had been in training with their battalion since leaving the village on August 5th, 1914, embarked from Liverpool aboard the 45,000 ton liner with 1000 ordinary ranks and 30 officers of the 1st/5th Battalion Norfolks (Territorials). They included Thornham's peace time sister company, the Sandringhams. At midnight the ship, escorted by destroyers, headed out into the Irish Sea.

The majority of the battalion had never faced an enemy in war. They were taken south, ferried ashore in Suvla Bay on the Gallipoli Peninsula on August 10th, and, with no time to acclimatize or prepare, were moved immediately into line and sent into the bloodiest of battles late in the afternoon of the 12th.

As one soldier from King's Lynn later wrote of that day: *At 3 pm we paraded, fixed bayonets and advanced … a day I shall remember as long as I live. We were soon in the middle of a hellish fire and men began to be hit. We kept on and on – nothing could stop us.*

Historians suspect that it was the glinting bayonets flashing in the burning sun that gave the Turks early warning of the coming attack. They were ready. After the attack, one local lad described the desperate situation that the Norfolk boys were placed in by muddled tactics, inadequate planning, lack of water and even the wrong maps.

We had to advance over two or three miles of open country under shell and rifle fire. The noise was terrific and the men were falling in large numbers. You see the Turks were on the side of a big hill among rocks and thick thorn bushes, so they had a great advantage. There seemed to be thousands of them. I got hit before we had gone very far and lay out in the sun for about two hours. Then I was taken to the Red Cross base and afterwards to a hospital ship. Quick work, wasn't it? In the peninsula for 48 hours and wounded. I don't know who else was hurt but I'm afraid there must be a great many...

Some of the deadliest fire of all was coming from green-painted teenage girl snipers hiding in trees.

During the early evening of that attack, the Battalion commander, Lt. Colonel Sir Horace Proctor-Beauchamp (ex-cavalry, late of the Sudan conflict and Boer War), pressed home an advance and took some of the battalion with him, including many Sandringham men. Their fate is well documented. Many died. Fortunately many more of the battalion were recalled before they too suffered the same fate.

Back in Norfolk, it was several days before the first news of what happened that day began to reach the village. It was only after the King asked for news of his Sandringham workers that the true horror of the attack emerged. It's still not possible today to say exactly how many died on August 12. But certainly many of the battalion's original officers were killed. Others were wounded. Captain Cedric Coxon, who had been with the Thornham men in the early days, was wounded and taken prisoner. As for ordinary ranks, perhaps as many as 300 of the original thousand 1st/5ths were killed or wounded on August 12/13th.

Thornham's Neville Helsdon was injured and returned home. Herbert Mitchell survived, only to be killed in another disastrous action in Palestine, the next port of call for the surviving 1/5th Norfolks.

As for Lance Corporal Robert James Tipple (20), son of butcher Billy and his wife Ellen, and Lance Corporal Frank Fenton (22), son of shell-fisherman Pennell and Elizabeth Fenton, they were not seen again. Their names are listed on Gallipoli's Helles memorial. It commemorates more than 20,000 Gallipoli casualties who had no known grave. The date of death inscribed beside the two men's names .... August 12, 1915 ... tells their story. Adie Tipple, one of Robert Tipple's sisters, never forgave Winston Churchill, the man responsible for the disastrous Gallipoli plan, for the death of her brother.

Footnote: It is possible that some of the wounded from the August 12/13 attack ended up recuperating at the Red House in the village. It is not surprising that some of the names of the nursing staff and other helpers there correspond with the names of soldiers fighting abroad ... including Tipple and Fenton.

The Western and Home Fronts

Thornham Regulars in the 1st Battalion of the Norfolks spent many months on the Somme and other Western Front battlefields. Six Siddle boys (Tim Siddle's father and five uncles) were in France. Three of them died. John William Potter, who had helped Nat Woods unload the *Jessie Mary* before the war, died of wounds on the Somme in 1916. Stafford Henry Imlach Bett, who had married Margaret Archdale, a member of the Hogge family, was wounded in the last few days of the war and ultimately lost most of one leg.

In Thornham, the first Women's Land Army helped out on the village farms. Mrs. Oswald Ames (The Manor) and Mrs. Bett (The Cottage) were offering farm training jobs for Land Army farm girls.

The sounds of war had come early to Thornham. In 1915 there was a famous Zeppelin Raid, when three of the flying machines flew along the coast from Great Yarmouth to King's Lynn, dropping bombs en route – including two on Sandringham.

George Hughes, grandfather to Neville Nudds who still lives in the village, told the local newspaper what he saw as one of those Zeppelin flew over Thornham.

I was just going to douse the lights and get into bed when I saw a sudden blaze. I looked up and saw a dark, long-bellied mass standing out against the dusky sky, and I knew it was a German airship. I saw it distinctly. I saw one bomb dropped and it exploded in Matthew Middleton's allotments which are behind my house. It made a hole about one foot deep by five feet in diameter.

Thornham schoolchildren were involved in raising money for the War Fund. In one week, Thornham schoolgirls raised £2-4-2d by collecting 530 Queen bees for Captain Victor Ames.

Another war had broken out in Thornham by 1917. The Parish Council received a Docking Rural District Council order to 'take steps for the destruction of sparrows'. Apparently they had reached plague proportions. Conservationists would like to have a few more today. The parish council called in Jack Sporne, the village 'vermin killer' to tackle the problem. Villagers were also paid 1½d per dozen for collecting sparrows' eggs.

Two sad footnotes to the war were the deaths in 1919 of Thornham's Royal Naval Air Service pilot, Flight Commander Peter Legh, the son of Major Gilbert Legh, who lived at Drove House, and submariner William Parnell, the 27 year-old son of William and Deborah Parnell.

Legh was wounded during the war, but recovered to take a civilian pilot's job. Peter was flying over Finchley in North London when his plane caught fire. A newspaper reported:

He tried to land, but, when several hundred feet from the ground, he leapt from the machine … some eyewitnesses say they saw Flight Commander Legh walk along one of the plane's wings. Holding up his flying dress to act as an improvised parachute, he took the leap which ended in his death.

William Parnell was one of the crew of the submarine L55, which was sunk in the Baltic during an engagement against a Russian Bolshevik naval force. Seven years later, the submarine was raised and the Russians returned the bodies of the 42 crewmen. The entire front page of the *Daily Mirror* of September 8th, 1928 was given over to the burial of the men in a single grave at the Royal Navy Cemetery at Haslar, Portsmouth.

Left: Charles Archdale had also served in the Boer War.

Right: A Christmas card from the front line.

Charles Archdale's last message home read: *It's no fun sitting in a trench but the longer I am here, the more I feel it is the only place for an able-bodied man and I wouldn't be anywhere else.*

The Archdale children in the 1890s. The boy on the left is Charles Archdale. The girl in the centre of the three girls is Mary. Excerpts from her diary about the family, and Charles' war service, can be read on the next two pages.

Charles Archdale, of the 7th Battalion, Norfolks, was killed by a sniper on the opening day of the First Battle of Cambrai in 1917. He was great-grandfather to Charles Rangeley-Wilson, currently living at The Red House with his wife Vicky. Stephen and Charles Bett's grandfather married Charles Archdale's sister Margaret, who is among those in the picture above.

Xmas Greetings

Ypres.
Neuve Chapelle
Festubert
7th. Loos. Division

Excerpts from Mary Archdale's diary

(by kind permission of Charles and Vicky Rangeley-Wilson).

March 27, 1914

Coz Eda (cousin Edith Ames Lyde, the Lady of Thornham Manor) *is dead suddenly in Shanghai – it seems almost unbelievable. Personally I have no cause to regret her, yet once I could have been very fond of her and we might have found some sympatiche* (sympathique) *– might have – never did – never can now…Thornham* (the estate) *is left to Father, then to Margaret and her son …*

August 2

…Germany has declared war on Russia

August 3

War declared on France and nearly everyone else …

August 5

Our Territorials (have) left … (probably talking about Edith Ames Lyde's Territorials who would soon be in Gallipoli))

December 1915

My brother Charley is still in England and now, thank Heavens, will not have to go to Gallipoli …

June 25, 1917

Baby Pleasance weeping, hands to eyes … Henry magisterial … baby has been naughty … (Pleasance Bett, aged about two, has pulled up a lavender plant)

November 29th, 1917

… a letter from France. Charley has been killed instantly. Fortunately Father was not looking … I went out of the room a minute or two, came back and got thro' breakfast somehow without his noticing anything. I went to tell the servants to bring no telegrams into the room. I walked up and down trying to be calm. After breakfast I tried to tell him – he was sitting reading peacefully. I couldn't and went up to Mrs. Patterson – in an emergency no one is kinder. She asked could she do anything – should she come back with me – and did so. Father was of course surprised to see her, it helped to warn him. I began, could not go on; she did, breaking it to him beautifully

… Father took it bravely. 'Ah, I knew I should never see him again,' he said piteously two or three times …

September/October, 1918
… we hear Hal (Stephen and Charles Bett's grandfather) is wounded in the ankle… Hal at Norfolk War Hospital. … has influenza and pneumonia … Hal decided to have his foot off.

A fellow officer in the 7th Battalion wrote to the family regarding Charles Archdale's death. *'His death was a tremendous blow to the regiment, as he was a top hole fellow, always as cool as a cucumber … he was shot dead by a sniper.'*

A Regimental War Diary entry shows that Charles Archdale had been wounded just three months before his death:

At 11.30 am today a hostile aeroplane flew very low over our lines, sweeping the front line parapet with machine gun fire. Captain C.W. Archdale and one man of C Company were wounded by bullets from the aeroplane. All rifles and Lewis guns were turned onto it without apparent result …

Mary did visit Cambrai after the war in search of her brother's final resting place. She was to learn that a temporary cemetery, where Charles' body had probably been placed, was totally destroyed in a German counter attack days later.

Mary sketched battlefield scenes in her diary on her post-war journey; this was done near Ypres.

Village Families in the '20s and 30s

Left: Mrs. Harriet Skeet (1870-1956), grandmother of Ellen Howell and great-grandmother to Robert (Holly), Leslie and Barbara Howell, and great-great grandmother to Beverley and Louise Howell.

Ellen Potter (born 1924), 'motors' up the High Street. Ellen's father Walter worked at Thornham ironworks.

Ellen's brother John (1929-1981) playing beach cricket with a relative, Charlie Bridges. Ellen's son Robert 'Holly' Howell was a good cricketer, and probably inherited Great Aunt Aggie's darts' skills too.

Aggie Potter (1884-1959) was known to all in Thornham as Aunt Aggie. Aggie's twin brother John (Jack) Potter (1883-1916) died on the Somme. A sad family story tells how John returned from the war for a single day's leave to marry his sweetheart, Maud Hines. He set off back to France that same day. They never met again.

Aggie Potter at the water pump.

Jane Bridges, Ellen Potter's other grandmother, standing outside Primrose Cottage. This house was also home to Aunt Aggie, a keen gardener and regular at the Chelsea Flower Show. She loved wild primroses and painted her front door the colour of those flowers; a colour that Marjory Webster, the current owner, still maintains.

Above: John and Mary Greef with their children. The youngest here is Alfred, who started the Thornham Greef dynasty. He arrived in the village in 1905 to work for Oswald Ames as a gardener at Thornham Manor.

Alfred Greef, who was employed in Thornham Manor gardens before the war, was wounded at Delville Wood on the Somme in 1916. The family tells a story of how, when he returned to work, he was told he would be paid less than his pre-war wages because his badly injured hand had left him debilitated. Alfred left and started his own business, a successful cycle repair shop.

Right: Clifford Grange outside The Red House. Clifford and his wife Evelyn were Eileen Richmond's parents.

Below: Ernest and Eliza (Dolly) Grange and their granddaugher, Eileen (later Richmond). The Grange Family lived in The Red House for a while. Ernest had several properties in Thornham. He built Lavender Cottage and The Laurels (later renamed Marsh Gate where Eileen and her second husband, Arthur 'Ricky' Richmond lived). Late in life, Eileen moved to another house in Staithe Lane but took the name Marsh Gate with her.

The Ames' car which they called *The Ghost*.

The end of the First World War brought huge social change. Working patterns changed. Women found new freedoms, and religious beliefs faced fresh examination after the slaughter of the First World War.

Perhaps that's why Thornham's new vicar, the Reverend Alfred Ellaby (1918-27) was campaigning to attract youngsters into church. Thornham local Ted Rason recalled the vicar offering 1½d (old pence) if a young parishioner attended all three Sunday services. The rate went down to 1d for two services and nothing for just one service.

The 1920s and 1930s were tough times for many, particularly farmers and farm workers alike. But the period saw older Thornham families still flourishing in the village, along with several new arrivals, including Reginald and Katharine ('Minnie') Rix who came to the village from Great Yarmouth in 1927. Reginald worked as gardener with the Reverend Hurrion Flowerdew Rushmer (1927-46).

Cyril Burt arrived from Hampshire in the 1930s and went to work as a butler/footman and chauffeur to Mr. Robarts at Thornham Manor. He didn't have to go far to meet his bride. Edith lived in a cottage just opposite the Manor. Cyril and Edith had 11 children, Gillian, Rita, Pauline, Eileen, Pam, Michael, Malcolm, Vivien, Robin, Colin and Andrew.

The Rix and Burt families would unite to produce one of Thornham's largest modern day families and a sporting dynasty.

A Towering Tale

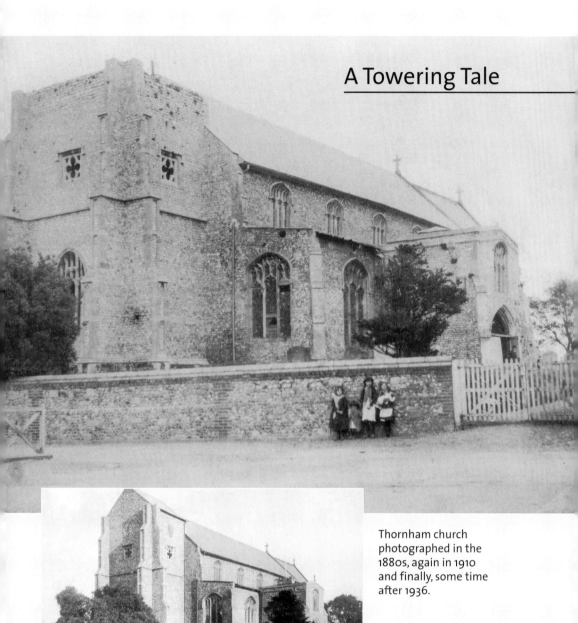

Thornham church photographed in the 1880s, again in 1910 and finally, some time after 1936.

6529   All Saints' Church, Thornham

The Incorporated Church Building Society

GRANTED £40, A.D.1903, TOWARDS RESEATING AND REPAIRING THIS CHURCH. UPON CONDITION THAT ALL THE SITTINGS ARE FOR THE FREE USE OF THE PARISHIONERS ACCORDING TO LAW.

Bryony Richmond and her father, Ricky. Bryony and Charles Carey were the first wedding couple to pass beneath the new lych-gate.

Tim Siddle and Henry Cobb built the church lych-gate.

Maggie Page (1894-1973), eldest daughter of Nathaniel Woods, opens the church lych-gate, built in memory of her father.

When Edward VII and Queen Alexandra visited Thornham in 1905, the King looked up at the church and observed: 'But you want a tower so badly'.

The original tower had collapsed in the 17th century and was never fully restored. For many years, the bell used to hang outside the church.

In 1907, the Vicar, the Rev. Nathan Waller, wrote in the Parish Magazine: *We have asked God if it is His Will to put it into the heart of someone to start the Tower Fund with £500. We have prayed this prayer for some three months. What God's will is we do not know … and now we leave the matter in his hands.*

It wasn't until 1936 that funds were raised to complete the upper part of the tower to mark the Silver Jubilee of King George V.

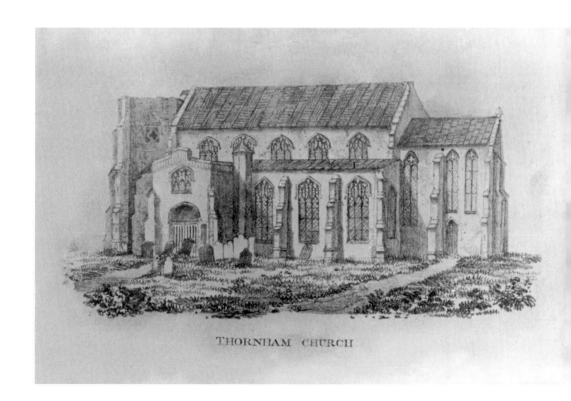

THORNHAM CHURCH

Grandpa Asker

Above: Robert and Mary Ann Asker

Margaret Bunkle's parents, Jane Elizabeth Asker (b. 1879) and Herbert John Bunkle (b. 1878) on their wedding day.

Robert Asker, seen here mowing the churchyard at the turn of the 20th century.

The day Robert Asker killed a rabbit on a Sunday brought about an unusual religious conversion.

Robert, grandfather to Dick, Mary, Lea, Janie, Maude and Margaret Bunkle, had been a Methodist Church preacher for many years. One Sunday, Robert, accompanied by his wife Mary Ann, had been on his way to a preaching engagement when he spotted a rabbit in a meadow. He took out his catapult and killed the creature.

When he got to his engagement, he was told he had been seen and couldn't preach at the chapel because he had killed on a Sunday. Robert protested, to no avail, that he was only providing food for his family. Robert vowed never to attend chapel again and joined Thornham Church where he became Sexton. His wife Mary Ann remained with the chapel for the rest of her life.

There is another Asker connection in Thornham churchyard; the weeping ash growing over the grave of a German seaman, Robert Krull. He died in a shipwreck in 1892 and his body had been washed ashore on Thornham Beach.

Margaret Bunkle, says that her grandmother, Mary Ann Asker was known as a village 'bringer in' and 'taker out'; in other words, before the days of everyone being able to afford midwives, doctors, nurses and undertakers, she was an unofficial midwife and also laid out the dead before the funeral.

So Mary Ann, with a farm horse and tumbrel cart, rode down to the beach and collected the body. Robert Krull was then buried in the churchyard. Margaret Bunkle recalls: 'I remember my mother telling me that granny planted that ash over his grave.'

Mary Ann Asker brought Neville Nudds into the world and later taught Neville's mother Beattie the skills of her special calling. Today Neville, in a kindly gesture towards past connections, tends the Bunkle graves in the churchyard.

Margaret Bunkle herself had an important 'home front' role in the Second World War running the Hunstanton telephone exchange and training men from the Signals Corps to set up exchanges in France after the D Day landings.

Later in life, Margaret was woken very early at home by a member of the night staff at Hunstanton Exchange and warned she might be needed at work. It was the morning of the 1953 flood! Her abiding memories are of hurrying into work and having a cup of tea that tasted foul. The sea water had got into the water supply.

Harvest Home

Above: Stacks at Manor Farm. The near figure is probably Ted Sutherland, Richard Heading's cowman. The boy on the left could be Ted's son, Noel. The building on the left is now part of Manor Farm Cottages.

Gathering up the straw by floodlight.

A horse elevator working after dark

Thomas Jones, great-grandfather of Daphne Siddle, Rita (Browning), Aubrey (Sadler) and Sandra (Rutland), with one of his horses.

In the old days, farm workers would celebrate the end of harvest by electing a Lord of the Harvest. He would lead the procession which carried the ceremonial corn dolly back to the farmhouse. There it would stay until the following year's harvest.

There were farm harvest suppers held in Thornham Drill Hall after the Second World War but even that tradition soon died out.

As Pleasance Bett, born in 1915 and sister of the late Henry Bett, says: 'Times have changed so much. Today it seems that one day you see a field of wheat growing and the next moment it's a field of stubble.'

It's not known exactly where in Thornham the floodlit pictures on the preceding pages were taken. Floodlights were used on occasions for night work to hurry up the 'harvest home'.

The first photograph, on page 72, shows a field already harvested and the men are now raking up loose straw left behind. The man below the wagon is the 'pitcher'. The two men on top are 'loaders' and, depending on which dialect you're talking, the young fellow in front of the horse is the 'hol'gee' or 'hold-yee' boy. The expression was used by the boy as a warning to those on top of the wagon that he was about to move the horse on and that they should 'hold on'.

The second photograph shows straw being raised onto the stack by a horse elevator. The horse (in the shadows) was attached to a pulley and walked around in circles, so driving the elevator. The youngest boys had the job of keeping these horses moving. Once a boy proved proficient at this job, he could be promoted to 'hol'gee boy'. Neville Nudds always thought it was rather cruel for a horse to be doing that job all day.

Break time

Harvest was hard, labour-intensive work for the farm workers of old, but the photograph opposite captures the romantic image of harvest time as the men rest.

'Harvest time was such fun in the old days,' says Pleasance. 'All those lovely horses. Life was so much slower. Harvest was the height of the year. We'd all go down to the harvest fields and have tea with the men. And you'd hear those beautiful Norfolk accents. There was such a lovely twang to it. But it's all gone now ... and who goes to the harvest field today?'

Ellen Howell remembers chasing rabbits with a stick as the harvesters moved in to clear the last cut of a field. There were also lots of picnics when the weather was good.

There were once several farms in the village: The Hall and Manor farms were tenanted by the Heading Family. The Betts farmed Malthouse, Jones'(or Old) and Ling farms. Vic Helsdon had the Dairy Farm. Other farmers included Ossie Waterfield, Joe Hines and Herbert and Matthew Middleton.

Manor Farm before conversion.

New Generations

Above: The infants in the 1930s.
Back row, (l-r): Mrs. Stevenson, the next two unidentified, Billy Rumbellow, Gordon Nudds, George Raven and Sam Hewitt.
3rd row: Freddie Coulson, unidentified, Joyce Smith, the next three unidentified, Vera Walker, Rene Plume, unidentified, Pat Middleton and Olive Whiting.
2nd row: next three unidentified, Doris Bell, next two unidentified, Joan Siddle, Lilly Siddle, Hazel Hooks, Rene Woods, D. Williamson.
Front row: ? Russell, L. Williamson, next two unidentified, ? Corston, Peter Tipple, next two unidentified, Henry Helsdon, C. Fenton, Fred Raven, Harry Smith, B. Groundsell.

Opposite: Animal Day at Thornham School in 1937.
(l-r) Back row: Leslie Williamson, Brian Groundsell, Audrey Myhill, Hazel Hooks, Hazel Bussey, Margaret Barnes, Freda Williamson, Joan Siddle, Joan Loose, Peter Tipple, Henry Greef, Cecil Rix and Neville Stimpson.
Middle: Tommy Rout, Stanley Eke, Leslie Crown, Noel Sutherland, Dick Sutherland, Nora Sadler, Jean Helsdon, Doris Whiting, Kathy Potter, Ellen Potter, Gerald Eke, John Bell, Margaret Bell and Cyril Mann.
Front: Doris Bell, Eddie Rix, Joan Roper, Pat Everett, Joan Sadler, Alan Sadler, Eric Green, Cynthia Filby, Shirley Stevenson, Derek Rush, Colin Corston, Daphne Sadler, John Potter, and Harry Hewitt.
Sitting: Velma Gilding, George Hewitt, Neville Nudds and Esme Ricketts.

Above: Another school photograph of the period.
Back row (l-r) unrecognised, David Wilson, Ronnie Wadlow, Michael Crown, Colin Corston, Mrs. Stevenson; middle: David Sutherland, Valerie Farmer, next two unidentified, June Rason, Bobbie Bocking, Alwyn Burrell; front: Michael Greef, Brian Sutherland, Nelia Cornell, Doris Wadlow, unidentified, Tony Whiting and Beryl Siddle.

Above: The juniors of the mid 1930s.
Back row: Miss Rout, Leslie Williamson, ? Russell, Brian Groundsell, George Raven, ? Overson and Harry Smith.
2nd row: Doris Bell (later a Smith), Hazel Bussey (later a Newman), Hazel Hooks, Lilly Siddle (later a Parker), Audrey Myhill and Joan Loose.
3rd row: Margaret Barnes, Freda Williamson, unidentified, Ellen Potter (later a Howell), Joan Sadler, Joan Siddle and unidentified.
Front: Gordon Russell, Peter Tipple, Sidney Raven, Russell Harwood (Thornham opening cricket bowler in the making), Cyril Fenton, Graham Raven and Bobby Corston.

Mrs. Ames Lyde appears to have started the Christmas party tradition when every child was given a present. Frank Gill continued the tradition in the years before the Second World War. Mr. Gill lived at The Laurels (later Marsh Gate). The photograph shows Mr. Gill on stage as Father Christmas with his daughter Nancy, a professional ballerina. Doris Smith (née Bell), a teenager at the time recalls: 'Mr. Gill financed these parties and gave a present to every child there. Oswald Waterfield from the Lifeboat Inn was the comedian, and the vicar, the Reverend Rushmer always did recitations.'

Polly and Dolly ... Polly Middleton, who lived at Oldfield Farm, and Dolly Able, who came to the village when she was only a few weeks old. Polly married a Mitchell and Dolly (right) tied the knot with a soldier, 'Jimmy' Bird.

Left: The class of 1939
(l-r) Back row: George Hewitt, Bobby Bocking, Cyril Mann, Tim Siddle, Freddie Eke, Eric Green, Bruce Wilson, Neville Nudds and teacher Miss Rout.
Mid row, Peggy Cornell, Barbara Williams, Margaret Bell, Daphne Sadler, Joan Roper, Joyce Wadlow, Gerald Eke, John Bell and Trevor Williams.
Front, Esme Ricketts (Robbie Wright's mother), Ronnie Corston, Shirley Stevenson, Ilene Ricketts, Betty Eke, Joy Matthews, Alan Sadler and Desmond Greef.

If you read Thornham School's punishment book for the 1920s and 30s, you might think the children were quite well behaved. Punishment entries were reasonably few and far between.

Henry Greef was at school during this time when Stephen (John) Stevenson was headmaster. 'He did keep strict discipline and he was a clever man. He taught us the Greek alphabet, and Euclid, the elements of geometry. But he did have his moods.'

Perhaps he was in a mood on that day in 1926 when several boys got punished; a 12 year-old boy got three strokes on the seat for being *lazy and idle*. Another boy of the same age got four strokes for being *lazy every lesson*. A third got *three plus two strokes on seat* for being *lazy and idle, disobedient'*.

On another day a young boy was punished for *rolling his eyes in class*.

The school at this time had three mixed classes. Mr. Stevenson ran the seniors, his wife the infants and Miss Rout the juniors. The school had over 100 pupils.

'Mr. Stevenson was very strict,' remembers Ellen Howell (née Potter). 'You could walk into class and hear a pin drop. I think there was a fair bit of caning. The boys got the cane. We had our hands rapped. "Hold your hand out girl!" That's what they said. I had a bit of a stutter and I'd be put in the corner for that.'

Ellen's classmate Doris Smith (née Bell) remembers her own habit of studying with her head quite low to the desk. 'Mr. Stevenson would pull up my head. But he had this discipline and we respected him for it – something that's missing today. Mr. Stevenson took the seniors but he was in overall charge. He would go into each class and see that everything was as it should be.'

Doris had a long school day. After school, she helped out at the Chequers Inn, which was then run by her uncle, Eddie Bell.

Ellen worked for the Stevensons during the holidays. 'I still called him Mr. Stevenson then. I wouldn't dare call him anything else. His wife taught the infants. She was ever so nice. The third teacher was Miss Rout. She lived to the age of 90 and she would come and visit us after she left the school. We liked her very much.'

Ellen, Doris and another friend in their class, Hazel Bussey (later Newman), were all about 15 years old on the eve of war. They agree that this was a wonderful period of their lives, dressing up for dances, courting and just being teenagers.

'In a lot of ways it was the best time for us,' says Doris. 'There were pageants, garden fêtes, and lots of dances. Most of the men could do ballroom dancing then. I remember George Hines, who joined the submarines in the war. He was a wonderful dancer.'

'Yes,' said Ellen, 'and you could go from one end of the village to the other and name every one. Someone lived in every house in those days.'

Daphne Siddle (née Sadler) agrees. 'You can't imagine the difference between then and now.'

Dolly Able was a teenager at the start of the war. She told Keith Skipper on BBC Radio Norfolk how, looking back to those days, she pictured herself 'rolling marbles up the road to school' (suicidal to try it today) and going on days out to Ringstead Downs with 'fourpence in her pocket'.

Dolly went to work as a house parlour maid for Miss Ames. The wages, she received were just six shilling a week. Later in life, she spent several years working on one of Thornham's mushroom farms.

Mr. Stevenson, the schoolmaster, didn't suffer fools gladly. In 1946, a Parish Council minute records that he told a heckler in the audience to 'go back to Holme where he belonged. '

He may not have known it, but his pupils named him 'Johnny', after his middle name.

Major David Jamieson (seen here in later years with his long-serving batman Harry Flatt,) won the Victoria Cross while leading his men in an almost suicidal defence of the Orne Bridgehead soon after the D-Day landings. The medal, he always said, was won by his men. Brenda Flatt, one of Harry Flatt's daughters still lives in the village.

Opposite: Thornham man George Hines was a Chief Petty Officer in submarines and the winner of the DSM (Distinguished Service Medal). It's thought that George joined the Royal Navy as a boy seaman in the early 1930s. He went into the Submarine Service in 1938 and served throughout the Second World War on several vessels, including *Otway, Upright, Sea Rover, Storm* and *Tantivy*. Later he was based at *HMS Dolphin*, the Gosport submarine depot. After the war he was a familiar figure in the Lifeboat Inn, with a constant companion, his dog Sadie.

Jim Tipple, a former village blacksmith, gave Mary (left) and Maude Bunkle witch hazel twigs, a traditional good luck talisman, when they left Thornham to serve in the ATS (Auxillary Territorial Service) in London.

Their sister Margaret recalls: 'He said they would be safe if they kept their twigs. It's one of those strange things really, but somehow Mary's disintegrated and Maude kept hers.'

The two girls were caught in a bomb raid on London's Chelsea Barracks in 1940. Mary died, but Maude survived unharmed. The army regiment, based in Thornham at the time, gave Mary a moving military funeral in the churchyard, with six bearers firing a salute over her grave.

Brother Dick Bunkle won the Military Medal after Dunkirk in 1940 when the Royal Norfolks were trying to reach St. Valery-en-Caux, the only place still open for evacuation. He was eventually captured along with many other Royal Norfolks, including Henry Bett, Harry Monks and George Walker. Tragically Charlie Goff, a pre-war Thornham footballer, was killed during these events.

Eileen Richmond (right) seem here in her pre-war nursing days. In 1939 Eileen married RAF pilot John Humphreys. Tragically, he was killed in a plane crash on the eve of their first wedding anniversary. Eileen became a Land Army girl during the war and later married Arthur 'Ricky' Richmond, who ran one of Thornham's mushroom farms.

Ian Hopper (right) with Henry Cobb soon after the war.

IN LOVING MEMORY
OF
IAN KENNETH
HOPPER
25-5-1912 13-5-1991.
A BRAVE MAN.

Ian Hopper's memorial stone in Thornham churchyard

Englishman Ian Hopper was living in Normandy in France with his wife Paulette when the Germans arrived in 1940. This was a period of the war before any real resistance movement had been organised.

This extraordinary man, apparently without any connections to the British secret services, began a one-man campaign of terror against the invaders; arson, sabotage and assassination. He became a highly efficient killer, especially of high-ranking Nazis and French collaborators.

Following his killing of a police chief in Caen in 1941, Ian and Paulette escaped to Paris, but soon after they were caught in an ambush in a café. Paulette died and Ian, badly wounded, managed to escape.

He was finally captured in the summer of 1942, suffered beatings and torture, and spent the rest of the war in various concentration camps including, finally, Dachau. But he survived and returned to England where he settled in Thornham and set up a mushroom farm.

A tall man, he was a familiar figure with his trade-mark French beret. He remarried and his widow, now Mrs. Diana Bett, still lives in the village.

Ellen Howell (née Potter) and Gwen Watson in their Red Cross Uniforms. Many Thornham girls joined the Thornham Red Cross, then organised by Mrs. Bett to provide first aid training. Ellen says: 'I still hadn't earned my red cross when this picture was taken.'

Below: This picture is unidentified. Was it a Thornham Remembrance march past?

An early invasion of 17 young evacuees from London marked the beginning of the war in Thornham. They came with their own teacher, who was quickly christened by the Thornham children 'scratchy bum'. In 2006, some of those surviving evacuees still write to their Thornham families.

The Helsdon, Sporne, Sutherland, Whiting, Bunkle, Middleton, Raven, Bett, and Nudds families were among those who took in London evacuees. The extreme poverty of some of the youngsters surprised the Thornham villagers, who, although hardly well-off themselves, seemed wealthy by comparison.

The serious and imminent threat of invasion in 1940 produced several deadly serious but slightly *Dad's Army* scenarios. On Granary Road, an explosive charge was laid in a pipe. Pleasance Bett remembers it. 'Of course, how could the Germans take England when Thornham had a bit of explosive placed in Granary Road. It was a morale booster.'

Daphne Siddle recalls how old farm vehicles were parked zig-zag fashion outside her birthplace, Jones Farm, to slow down any invading Nazis.

Before the Second World War, it had been usual for village girls leaving school to enter domestic service, while the boys tended to go to work on the land. At the outbreak of war, three young Thornham school-leavers, Ellen Potter (later Howell), Doris Bell (later Smith) and Hazel Bussey (later Newman) had entered domestic service with, respectively, the Seymours of Stanhoe, the Robarts at Thornham Manor and the Jamiesons of Drove House.

But it wasn't for long. The war effort took precedence on the labour force because farm and munitions workers were desperately needed. Ellen went to war at Ringer's farm in Titchwell. Doris joined a munitions' factory in Norwich (later working on a Bett's farm) and Hazel ultimately worked on the same farm. Ellen remembers how they were allowed to glean the harvest fields for corn to feed to the chickens.

Doris met her future husband, Peter, among the soldiers who came to the village. Ellen met her husband-to-be at the same time. She recalls working in a field one day when a companion pointed to a man in the opposite field. 'She told me to go and ask him what the time was,' recalls Ellen. 'So I popped through the hedge and asked him.'

A few days later she was cycling nearby and met the man again. He was George Howell. 'He stopped and spoke to me,' recalls Ellen, 'and asked if I'd go for a bike ride with him. I said I would if I could get father's permission.'

A courtship proceeded and the couple eventually married after the war. Hazel Bussey met Jack Newman, her soldier and husband-to-be, while walking in Hunstanton with a friend a couple of weeks before the D-Day landings in 1944. They got talking and kept in touch after the war. They married in 1949.

Back in the early days of the war, the beach had been lined with anti-tank defences and mines were laid in many locations. The army had moved into the village in force too. The military took over Thornham Manor (HQ Army), The Laurels, Marshlands, Bay Tree Cottage (officers), York House (WRVS canteen) and King's Head (accommodation for officers' wives).

Up on the Ling (Lyng) Common, artillery units were set up for shooting practice. The gunners' targets were on Thornham beach. Soon, twenty-five pounder shells were regularly whistling over the village, some occasionally dropping short. Henry Greef recalls the windows of the Post Office being blown out by an air burst, and Tim Siddle remembers part of Jamieson's hedge being blown to bits by another 'short'.

Church services at this time were sometimes interrupted by officers hurrying into the church and climbing up the tower to begin shell spotting duties. There was no danger of the spotters being deafened by bells. The ringing of church bells was reserved as a warning that the country was being invaded.

In July 1940 a Hampden bomber crashed on New (Ringstead) Road. The crew survived. As youngsters, both Cecil Rix and Tim Siddle remember hearing the crack of the aircraft's unspent live ammunition going off in the flames. First World War veteran Alfred Greef banned his son Henry from visiting the crash site until 'the plane had cooled'. In September the following year, Henry managed to clamber into the cockpit of another Hampden bomber which crashed on Thornham Common. Running out of fuel after a bombing mission was something that happened occasionally.

Noise levels increased with the later creation of a tank firing range on Titchwell beach. Tim Siddle and Henry Greef recall how swerving tanks made short shrift of the gates on Thornham's Green. Tim says that, later on, wayward Bren Gun carriers and military vehicles often knocked the old village about a bit.

Tim Siddle's father Sam, a First World War veteran, was one of the special constables in Thornham at this time. He often went out with fellow 'special' Arthur Back, checking that everyone was keeping a total black-out.

Pleasance Bett, like several Thornham people, found herself on service away from the village. Trained by the local Red Cross, she was called up as a VAD (Voluntary Aid Detachment). She was working on a ward in a military hospital when she was given the news that her brother Henry had been captured and was now a prisoner-of-war. She remembers her response vividly. 'I burst into tears and I heard a patient say: "Bad news, nurse?" I said "No, not really. I suppose it's good news." I was just relieved to hear that he was alive and safe. Henry was a prisoner of war for five years.'

Pleasance became a *Fany* (First Aid Nursing Yeomanry) and was then drafted into Bletchley Park, encoding and decoding secret messages for and from SOE agents in France. She served in the Far East too. Also in the Nursing Yeomanry was Joan Ames, who flew back with the wounded after D-Day.

Thornham Women's Institute played its part on the home front. Its wartime President was Mrs. Robarts, of Thornham Manor. The vice-presidents at the time were 'Mesdames Ames, Bett and Porcher'. The committee was 'Mesdames Helsdon, Rushmer, Lee, Richards, Welsh, Baker, Wilson, Greef, B. Smith (Holme), Joan Hart (Holme), J. Potter and Misses Tipple, Sporne and Bays.' The Entertainment Committee consisted of three pianists: 'Mesdames Back, Greef and Wilson.'

The Thornham Roll of Honour includes Mary Elizabeth Bunkle (ATS) died 1940; Corporal Eric Howling, Royal Norfolk Regiment, died 1947; Pilot Officer David Druce, RAF died 1940; John Humphreys, RAF, died 1940, Samuel Hewitt (23), RAF Volunteer Reserve, died 1946; Eric Porcher, 28, died Sicily 1943, and Donald Woods (28), a great nephew of Nathaniel Woods, died in Belgium 1944.

The war had changed Thornham. It was no longer the isolated Norfolk village it had been. Young Tim Siddle discovered that. Tim, who had hardly travelled more than a few miles from his birthplace, found himself in faraway Norwich, minus his clothes and being inspected for National Service duty by an army medical officer. A while later the village's latest National Serviceman took centre stage in world affairs as he boarded a Dakota transport to take part in the Berlin airlift.

'Cubby ho, cubby weesh!'

Samuel Jones, grandfather of Daphne Siddle (née Sadler), Rita (Browning), Aubrey (Sadler) and Sandra (Rutland), takes a pair of his horses to drink in the pond just opposite Jones' (or Old) Farm on the main road into the village.

Samuel Jones and his wife Sarah.

Below, left: Colvy Jones, mother of Daphne, Rita, Aubrey and Sandra .

Below: Daphne Siddle as a child.

Luan Walker, driving a tractor and reaper-binder. The registration number, BPW, chalked on the grille, is a Norfolk one.

George Bell achieved fame when he safely delivered these calf triplets. The drama occurred in one of the now demolished Malthouse Farm barns. George was father to Doris (later Smith), and grandfather to Chris, Richard, David, who sadly died recently, Alison, Julie and Jeanie.

'George was on television and radio and in farmers' magazines,' recalls Doris. 'He actually had to give the weakest calf the kiss of life.

He stayed with them all night and had spent so much time nurturing the pregnant beast that his wife, Ethel, told him he ought to move into the barn!'

Left, top: Joe Bush, who was foreman for Henry Bett from 1947 until the 1960s, was taught to drive on the farm. On the first day of lessons from Henry, Joe got his boots caught up between accelerator and brake pedals. Having spent most of his working life with horses, he did what came naturally. He pulled back on the steering wheel and cried out: 'Whoooaa!'.

Above: Hugh Andrew about to set his ferret on the trail of a rabbit in the 1970s. The ferret had a transmitter on its neck so it could be located if it got lost underground. Other gamekeepers who worked for Thornham Farms included Walter Gent (and underkeeper John Bell), Tom Browning, Billy Moulton and John King. John and Rose King's son Mervyn became an international indoor bowls champion in 2006.

Below: Thornham Farms' Tug-o-war team ... (l-r) Maurice Chapman, Luan Walker, Pat Sutherland, Frank Edge, Dick Spurdon and George Walker.

Left: Jack Middleton and other workers at Ian Hopper's mushroom farm.

Left: Henry Bett, father to Stephen and Charles, back home after five years as a prisoner of the Germans. 'Quite frankly' he said later 'when I got back, I had to drag Thornham Estate from the 19th century into the 20th. My son is taking it into the 21st. He does ask my advice but doesn't necessarily take much notice of it.' Henry died in 1995.

Right: Stephen and Charles on a combine harvester in 1958.

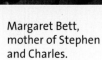

Margaret Bett, mother of Stephen and Charles.

Charles and the late Christina Bett and their children, Zoey, Peter, Neil and Joey.

Eric Beck in 1942 before going to
the Far East with the Royal Norfolks
and, later, in his 'demob suit'.

Eric Beck, who spent 43 years at Thornham Farms, worked on a Choseley farm before the Second World War. When he returned to that village after the war, he renewed his acquaintance with an old friend called Daisy, one of the farm horses.

'The farm had a tractor by then,' he remembers. 'so I was surprised to see that they'd kept Daisy. Anyway there was a field to be hoed and I said to the foreman that Daisy could do the job. He looked at me strangely and said: 'Who the hell do yer think's going to lead that hoss all day? We can't afford to do it that way.' Well bugger that, I said, I'd do it.'

So Eric harnessed up Daisy and led her off.

'I put her to work,' he recalls. "Off you go," I'd say. She walked between those rows of beet perfectly. "Come on my ol' beauty" I'd say. Sometimes depending on the slope of the land, I'd call out: "Lean over a bit! Lean over, yew ol' bugger! Cubby ho. Cubby ho!" That brought her round to the left. And when we got to the head of the field, I'd say: "Hold it, old girl." Then I'd pull down the hoe handle and lift up the halters. "Weesh! Cubby weesh!" That brought her round to the right. "Come on round, you big bugger. Come round girl. Come on, my old beauty. Weesh! Weesh! Weesh! Weesh!" The horse would turn gently in stages until she was facing back down the field again. "Wo back! Wo-back!" Then she's ready and I'd set the hoe up again and off we'd go. "Walk on. Git on, gal." '

'We'd do another row and I'd talk to her as we went down the field. "Just finish the row old girl, and then we'll have a break at t'other end. I'll get yew some grub and water." I always brought up a water cart when I was workin' a horse and a bag of oats and chaff (cut cornstalks) for a feed. I'd get a bucket of water and say: "Want a drink old mate?" She'd have a drink and off we'd go again. I loved old Daisy alright. She was a beautiful little mare, a beautiful little old thing. After that first job, I went to take her out again. The foreman, he laughed: "What? You're going to take her out again?" "Yes," I said. They all laughed. But she did the job alright.'

'I loved horses,' said Eric. 'I got that from my father who was a horse teamer. They were the men who looked after the various teams of horses. Each horse team might be special. Different horses did different jobs.'

When Eric came to work for the Bett family in 1946, they still had horses at Malthouse Farm. Charlie Whiting, grandfather to Tony, who lives in the village today, was one of the farm's 'teamers' then.

The 'teamers', although better paid that the ordinary farm workers, had the longest working day. They started work at five, a couple of hours before the others, to feed and water the horses. Then they had their own breakfasts before returning to take the horses out to work. 'You'd never take a horse out without giving it a feed,' says Eric.

It would be late in the day before the teamers could bed down the horses for the night and put their own feet up.

Thornham Pubs

The King's Head

Below: The King's Head lit up. In 1946 the Parish Councillors bemoaned the fact that the lights of the King's Head were the only ones that helped villagers see their way up the High Street. It would be another five years before street lighting came to Thornham.

7291 King's Head Entrance, Thornham

Landlord John George Parrinder Wilson, 1937 – 57.

Below: (l-r) Lenny 'Bishy' Mann, Keith Bird, Ivy and Reg Needham and Dudley 'Duxie' Batterbee. Reg and Duxie met for the very first time on a job at Sedgeford railway station just after the war. Duxie, for some reason, muttered a couple of words in Italian. Reg knew instinctively where Duxie had learned the lingo, just as he had. It turned out that Reg (RAF) and Duxie (Royal Norfolks) had been just miles apart in Italy during the wartime advance on Rome. They stayed excellent friends ever after. The photograph here was taken before the entrance to the new indoor toilets was built.

Doris Smith (née Bell) in the King's Head kitchen with
the landlord Roger Fitz Patrick, and chef Jozef Partyka,
father of Michael, who, with his wife Jenny, now runs
the best mobile fish and chip shop on the coast.

TARIFF

WEEKLY TERMS............from 10 gns per person
BED & BREAKFAST............from 25/- per person
MORNING TEA................1/- single 1/6 double
AFTERNOON TEA....................3/6 per person

LUNCHEONS & DINNERS
also à la carte menu

Own garden produce, local sea foods when in season
Hot and cold water & electric fires in all bedrooms

Garage and spacious car park

Early 1960s menu from the time of landlord
John Houghton.

The King's Head is perhaps the village's oldest pub. Records suggest that it has been around since at least 1641.There used to be a leaded window in the pub on which someone had scratched the words: *J. Horne put me here and bid me stand for many a year. 1771.* The pub is also marked on Faden's 18th-century map.

George and Ida Wilson were the celebrated hosts here before and after the Second World War.

George grew up in Ringstead, where his father was a farmer. He ran away to fight in the First World War as a 16 year-old, claiming to be nineteen, and joined the Argyle and Sutherland Highlanders. He was taken prisoner in Germany.

The pub may have changed its name, but the Thornham Ironworks sign from the 1900s survives.

He took over the pub in 1937 and was a regular member of the Parish Council. An enthusiastic supporter of the Royal British Legion, George was also involved in the Second World War; first with the local Brancaster Home Guard, and then in Europe as a member of the Royal Army Service Corps. Ida ran the pub while he was away on service.

The couple, who between the wars were founder members of Hunstanton Tennis Club, had three children, Bruce, Mollie and David. The latter married Reg Needham's daughter Doreen. George died in 1957 and Ida in 1979.

Major Roger Fitz Patrick, who followed the Wilsons, introduced a 'Puffa Bar', which catered for children while the grown-ups were in the main bar.

The pub was renamed the Orange Tree in 2004 but still boasts an old King's Head sign made at Thornham ironworks.

Former landlords of the pub also include William Platten (1830s), Charles Rust (1840s), Joseph Crane (1851-1896), Samuel Howard (1900-08), Frank Callaby (1912-1916), Arthur Patrick (1920s), Charles Dixon (1925-37), John Houghton (1962-70), Gerry Camkin, Tony Cook and Jake John.

The Chequers Inn

The Chequers Inn circa 1910. Its earlier name was the Chequers Commercial Inn.

Not much had changed by the 1950s.

(l-r) Butcher Harry Wyett, Billy Howard, Tony Petchey, Reg Needham, Bobbie Bocking, Benny Howard and Randall Pearce.

Richard Sidey and his dog Champagne.

One of several murals painted by a customer in the 1960s.

The Chequers Inn was reborn as the Old Coach House at the turn of the 21st century, an event which rather confused the postman … there were already village properties called *The Coach House* and *Coach House Lodge*.

The Chequers Inn was built around 1800. But it could be much older. Pevsner and Wilson in *The Buildings of England* date the oldest part of the building at circa 1680.

Richard Sidey and his wife Dorothy ran the Chequers Inn during the 1970s. They were very popular with locals, toffs and trippers alike. Richard wasn't known for ringing the bell to call time. A late drink was always a possibility. For modern generations reading this, the bell in past ages was rung to announce the pub was closing for the night.

During a farewell party to the Sideys, a tribute to ex-Navy man Richard was read out. It included these words:

We all thought Richard had hove to, dropped anchor for good. But quite suddenly, the old sea dog announced he was off to sail new oceans. And with that he actually rang the bell.

Reg (Needham) spoke for us, mourners all. 'It must be a fire,' he cried, 'Richard would never ring the bell to call time.'

Sadly it wasn't the pub burning down. We could have rebuilt that. No, the bell tolled for us ... and for Richard ...

They still say that the old Chequers Inn is haunted by another former landlord Les Tucker. He's blamed even today for the doors forever opening and shutting by themselves.

And if anyone hears a growling sound in the pub, you can be sure it will be old Billy Howard who's returned. There's a vent between what was the public bar and the old outside loos. He took great delight in howling through the vent when he was in the loo.

Doris Smith's uncle, Eddie Bell, landlord of the Chequers Inn before, during and after the Second World War, was a keen cricketer (See: Sporting Days). On match days in Eddie's time, the teams had tea at The Chequers and then continued playing into the evening. Thornham's tennis and bowls clubs also had a court and green behind the Chequers in the 30s/40s.

Other landlords include John Grice (1830s), William Allen (1845-1883), Robert Allen (1888-1890), Frederick Savage (1891-1908), James Page (1912), Benjamin Watson (1916-1929), Will Scrowther, George Edgeley (early 50s), Bill Higgins (50s), Samuel 'Les' Tucker, (until 1970), Nick and Patsy Martin, Geoff and Cathy Cambridge and, under its new name, Patti Gambling and Tania Rowell.

The Lifeboat Inn

The Lifeboat Inn during the 1920s
with the farm sheds opposite.

Right: The Lifeboat in
the 1950s, during the
Bullard's era.

The Hogge family was never far from a pint of their own ale whenever they came down to Thornham Hall from Lynn, where they were prosperous merchants. They built The Red House and Thornham Hall. The inn sign shows that the Lifeboat was selling Setch Ales in this early photograph. Setch Brewery dates back to 1767 and was owned by George Hogge & Co. in 1836, according to White's Directory. It went through various changes of ownership before becoming Hogge and Seppings in 1863. Hogge and Seppings was sold to Bullard's in 1928, which was subsequently swallowed up in the Watney's conglomerate of the 1960s.

Olive and Oswald Waterfield, hosts at the Lifeboat Inn for many years.

Vincent Sadler and his wife Elizabeth. His mother was licensee at the end of the 19th century. Vincent lived to be 101.

The rear of the Lifeboat Inn before development.

Vincent Sadler, who lived to the grand age of 101, used to boast that he had been 'born in a lifeboat'. It was true.

Vincent, Alice and Mary Ann Sadler were the children of John and Elizabeth Sadler, who ran the Lifeboat Inn in the 1870s when it first became known by its current name.

Alice married Reuben Sylvanus Waterfield, who had the pub until 1950 when their son Oswald and wife Olive (née Chinery) took over. Vincent became a Brancaster baker and Mary Ann married the Dutch sailor Helmer Petersen, who came ashore from the wreck of the *Lydia*. (See: *Love, The Lydia and the Lifeboat Inn*).

Originally, the inn was probably a farmhouse. 18th-century maps show a building on this site in the days when a rough track lead from here directly to the village of (Old) Hunstanton.

Certainly, the pub's early drinking history was as a beer house. That probably meant a front room operation with the wife of the house serving beer and the husband out at work. Francis Pointer was an early licensee. He was followed by Thomas Birley.

Benny (brother of Billy) Howard used to say that during the early Waterfield days the pub had no glasses, just tankards. He added that the place had 'corn sacks for carpet and sold more milk than beer'. The Waterfields were listed in local trade directories as 'cowkeepers' and Ossie certainly used to deliver milk around the village.

The Waterfields were followed by, among others, Peter Scattergood, Clive Delino, Nick and Lynn Handley and Charles and Angie Coker (1995).

Left: By the 1950s, the Lifeboat had a thriving caravan site.

Just checking for comfort ... the new 'inside' ladies loos with Vera Goff and Daphne Siddle.

The Red Cow

This photograph shows the rear of the former pub.

The Red Cow was the first village pub to change its name … but that was nearly a hundred years ago.

The pub closed down at the turn of the 20th century soon after being renamed the Oak Inn. Oak House is now a private residence.

The first registered landlord of the Red Cow was Thomas Townshend (1845), followed by George Ivey (1865), John Whiley (1869), Frederick Flegg (1871), Mrs. Ann Flegg (1875-1883) and Isaac Flegg (1888-1892).

Thornham Hall

Thornham Houses

Thornham Hall. That's Reggie Baker mowing the lawn, and (below) as drawn for a 1778 planning map.

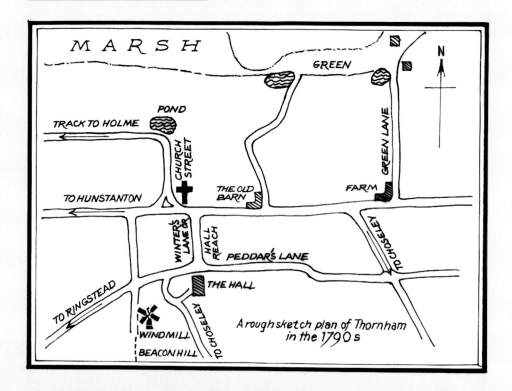

The gate at the end of Ship Lane (right) shows the line of an
old track (shown on the map above) that once led to Holme.

When 18th-century country landowners built themselves a new stately 'pile', they tended to rearrange the local road system to suit their needs.

The sketch of Thornham Hall comes from a 1778 plan showing road changes instigated when George Hogge, a wealthy Lynn merchant, had just completed the house. It appears from the plan accompanying the drawing that an old road previously passed immediately in front of the house.

The hall was nearly demolished in the 1950s. It was in such a bad condition that a more recent owner, Henry Bett, had considered pulling in down. But, finally, he decided to restore the house to its former glory.

The unusual feature on the roof was a look-out from where ships could be seen arriving in the harbour.

The rough plan of Thornham streets at the turn of the 18th century (which uses some elements of Faden's map) shows that the area around the Hall was an important road junction with tracks heading off to Ringstead, Choseley (via Peddars Lane), Docking and the village centre. It also shows that the way to the Green used to be via an old track that led off the High Street at the eastern end of the Old Barn, curling north to meet the Green between The Queen of Sheba Pit and an old property (probably the building that became *Casablanca*).

Old maps of Thornham, especially the 1843 tithe map, highlight some of the older village families; the Woods and Corston families dominate the properties around the eastern end of the Green at the time. Asker, Sadler, Francis, Sutherland, Jones, Middleton, Mitchell and Renaut are other familiar family names listed as living in various properties.

The 1843 map also lists some delightful but long-forgotten field names, including *Cowslip Pit Close*, behind Long Wood, *Pot Ladle* near the Ling, *Wheat Piece*, opposite the Lifeboat Inn, *Old* and *New Hungry Hill*, stony fields near the Choseley Road that take any amount of fertiliser but still don't grow much, *Chequers Pightle* (behind the old pub), *Hall Close* by the Hallow and *Upper* and *Lower Scull Close*, on the right up Choseley Road. (Close means a hedged or fenced piece of land and *pightle* is a small field or scrap of land).

The Red House has never been sold outside its original family owners (the Hogge/Archdale kinship). Currently, it's home to Charles Rangeley-Wilson (an Archdale), his wife Vicky and family.

Pevsner and Wilson put a date of around the 1770s on this building. Like Thornham Hall, also built for George Hogge, The Red House has a rooftop look-out used to spot ships arriving in Thornham Harbour.

The Grange Family (the late Eileen Richmond's relatives) lived here before the First World War. Evelyn Grange is seated extreme left; second from right, standing, is Mary Ann Asker.

During the war the house was a convalescent hospital. Nurses and helpers at the time included Tibby Smithbone, Aggie Potter, Eva Petersen, Ethel Sporne, Louise Proudfoot and Evelyn Grange.

Thornham Manor was a new property finished in 1904. It was built by Major Oswald Ames on the site of earlier buildings.

Oswald and his family lived here until the 1920s when Mr. John Robarts, a London banker, moved in. Mr. Robarts kept the place in style with a 'downstairs' team that included a butler, footman, under-footman, chauffeur, housekeeper, four housemaids (including Doris Cobb), several gardeners and a hall boy.

In the 21st century, the house was converted into three dwellings with other properties being built in the gardens.

Manor gardeners Lewis Mitchell and Stephen Hewitt.

The Cottage – a game of croquet in progress.

'Aunt Eda's moved on now,' says Pleasance Bett, talking of Mrs. Edith Ames Lyde who lived at – and allegedly haunted – the Cottage.

The manor-sized Cottage is one of the oldest properties in Thornham, with a 1624 date stone. Stephen and Charles Bett's father, Henry and his sister Pleasance were brought up here.

It was Henry who was convinced that 'Aunt Eda' haunted the place. Pleasance recalls him telling her of one incident.

'Henry was alone in the house when he heard someone going upstairs. There was a shuffling sound as though someone was hauling themselves up on the banisters. That was how Edith had climbed the stairs in later years because of her arthritis. Henry called out: "Who's there?" But there was nobody to be seen.'

Stephen says that his father experienced several such events.

In the 1970s, the property was sold and divided into two homes.

The Greef Family

Village postman Henry Greef during the winter of 1963.

Below: Thornham Air Training Corps in 1946.
Back Row: English, Bonamy, Carter, Peter Ginn, unidentified, Harry Hewitt, ? McGinn and Charlie McGinn.
Middle row: John Jarman, Henry Greef, Stevens, Mr. Crowther, Tommy Carter, unidentified and Bill Collison.
Front: Cecil Rix, whose brother John died in a bombing raid over Germany, and ? Barnard.

(l-r) Ronnie Fisher, Chris Smith, Gerald Harwood,
Henry Greef, Eric Edge (upper), Frederick Chapman,
Alan and Douglas Greef.

For a boy growing up in the 1940s, with Thornham's wartime skies crowded with bombers and fighters, it wasn't surprising that Henry Greef developed a lifelong interest in aircraft.

Henry was too young to serve in the war, but from 1944 onwards he was involved with the Air Training Corps, National Service in the RAF and Observer Corps. From those beginnings, Henry's Junior Observer Corps was born.

With the arrival of American A-bombers just down the road at RAF Sculthorpe in the 1950s, Thornham found itself on the front line of the Cold War. In reply to a request from someone looking for accommodation in the village then, the Parish Clerk wrote back saying: *Undoubtedly you are unaware that there is very little accommodation in this village as most of the houses or flats that do become vacant are let to Americans …*

From an operational HQ in an old wartime hut atop Dutchwoman's Hill, at the bottom of Shore Road, Henry Greef taught the youngsters of the Junior Observer Corps to recognise all the Russian, British and American aircraft.

Later he would teach them to track satellites, take them on trips to Heathrow Airport and show them around local air bases.

Henry still monitors satellites and all the aircraft that fly over Thornham from his own communication HQ, a very hi-tech garden shed. And the address of his house is *Hampden Cottage*, named after the Hampden bomber, one of which Henry visited after it crash-landed above the village in the Second World War.

Henry is a stalwart of village life in so many ways, like his father and mother before him. His mother Anna ran Thornham Post Office from 1936–1970. His father, Alfred, was a relief postman during the Second World War. Henry was the village's newspaper 'boy' and postman (1951–1968), before becoming postmaster himself in 1971, a role he continued in until 1986.

Henry is a great supporter of the Royal British Legion and a pillar of the local church, being a member of the Church Council and Deanery Synod. He also received the Maundy Money from the Queen.

Henry and his wife Joy had three children, Alan, Douglas and Stephen. Henry's brother Desmond, who was in charge of music at the Glebe School in Hunstanton for a long time, received an M.B.E. for services to music.

Footnote: Henry's guide to the village's postal history: in November 1814, a first Penny Post service was established at Brancaster with a receiving house organised in Thornham. By 1836, the village was getting its post from the Wells Mail Coach service. Mr. Sharpin is listed as the first post master in the village in 1845. He was succeeded by William Edwards, Edward Southerland, J. Edwards, T.E. Southerland, Howes Tipple and Cyril G. Ducker, son of the Thornham trader.

Left: Thornham's drapery and grocer's shop in the 1920s. W.R. Johnson went into partnership with Back after the First World War.

Above: The cows, passing the King's Head in the background, are probably on their way back from milking at Vic Helsdon's Dairy Farm to graze on the meadows by the Lifeboat Inn.

Another view of the shop with a horse and cart outside.

Where there's a will … there's often a bit of local history.

In 1784 widow Ann Taylor sold the property where Stocks Hill House and Johnson's Row now stand for £30 to merchant Henry Benton.

In 1804, Henry mentions in his will that he has a nephew called Joseph Benton, a man he describes as 'a linen draper in Manchester'.

Manchester would soon become the cotton centre of the world. So it seems that a small village draper's shop had a link with an important piece of social history.

By 1843 the property has been bought for £150 by another draper called William James. He left it to his daughter Emily Louisa, who married merchant James Johnson, probably the reason for the name of the cottages, Johnson's Row.

Emily and James left the business to their elder son, William Robert Johnson, who sold it in 1946 (including five Johnson's Row cottages then tenanted by the Leeder, Jones, Thompson, Nudds and Mann families).

Above: York House in the High Street was the location of an early butcher's shop, with the entrance to the slaughter yard behind.

Right: Thornham on the eve of the Second World War. Mrs. Greef's Post Office is on the left. Looking out of the doorway on the right are the three Hewitt brothers, Sam (behind) and Harry and George, the sons of Stephen Hewitt, who became head gardener at The Manor. That's Ginny Bustin by the wall. Her home (in Cobble Yard) and Jim Tipple's property (just before the Old Barn on the left) were among several village cottages later demolished. Frank Callaby's truck is in the far distance by the barn.

Daphne Siddle having a chat with Amy Wyett outside the butcher's shop. Amy's husband Harry was a great village character. They always said he 'served a sermon with his sausages'. His youngest son Mark later ran an antiques business from the premises.

Right: Thornham Market Place. The property on the right was a shop and delicatessen until the 1970s.

Left: The Ducker family outside London House, their Thornham home and also the location of their main shop. They are the founder, James William Ducker and his wife Jane, and their sons James and Cyril (with tennis racket). Their other three shops are shown above.

The Ducker sales team.

High Street, Thornham. (*Ducker's Series.*) J 2905.

The Ducker empire in the opening years of the 20th century was a veritable supermarket and shopping centre of its day.

Cloth by the yard, groceries, newspapers, heating fuel, hardware, drinks, chicken corn … they stocked it all. Holiday makers could even hire a horse and trap to ride down to the beach and buy a Ducker postcard to send home too.

James William Ducker and his wife (Sarah) Jane, launched the business. The main shop was at London House, where the Duckers lived, and the other shops were on the Church Street corner.

James and Jane had two sons, one also named James William, and Cyril. Cyril, was well known in the village as an excellent pianist and organist, who also had a dance band.

Irene Ducker, who married a grandson of the founder and now lives in Burnham Market, said: 'I remember my husband saying that he once had to work the church organ bellows while Cyril played the *Tiger Rag.*'

Cyril died young from TB, while James joined the Black Watch in Canada.

The barn on the village green was used by the Duckers as a warehouse. Later, Sonny Middleton and Oswald Waterfield stored corn here.

There was still a village garage until late in the 20th century.
This picture shows the staff in the 50s. (l-r) Len Farr, Bill
Jacobs, Ray Francis, Mary Jacobs, Jim Jacobs, Mrs. Jacobs
Senior, Jimmy Rix and Ronnie Scales. Other owners included
Vic Hardy and Sue Grout, Ken and Cath Hayward, Dave
Smalls, Bill Tollerton, Mr. King and Mr. Parker, and Noel
Gosling, who had the garage in the '30s and '40s.

The garage staff at work.

Puddings, Patties and Pies

The school meals team. Back row: Beattie Hunt, Daphne Sadler (later Siddle), and Maud Walker. Seated is Vera Goff (née Walker).

These girls look good on the diet .... Back row: (l-r) Gillian Burt (later Rix), Mary Rix (later Richrdson), Shirley Riseborough (later Lake), Marcia Burrell (later Thaxter), Pamela Crown (Seaman); front row: Marian Howling and Jenny Bell (later Kirby).

The class of 1951
Back row (l-r): Glynis Sutherland, Carol Druce (Oak House), Mary Bush, Janice Jongman, June Goff, Maureen Fenton, Diane Mann, Eileen Burt, Margaret Payne and Mrs. Stevenson; middle row: Shirley Mann, Maureen Crouch, Pamela Burt, Marilyn Williams, Ann Middleton, Veronica Cobb, Valerie Farmer, Sylvia ?; front row: Trevor Bird, Keith Bird, Lionel Francis, Clive Bell, John Jarred, Eric Francis, Roy Frohawk and Aubrey Sadler.

Shepherd's pie, meat patties, meat puddings and gravy, cheese pies and semolina with orange sauce and custard … just some of the items on the post Second World War school menu.

There were no school meals at Thornham until the late 1940s. Hazel Bussey (later Newman) was an early member of the kitchen team, as were the dinner ladies pictured left.

Daphne Sadler began helping with the preparation of school meals in 1948. In those days the Thornham team cooked a hundred or more meals each day because it also supplied Ringstead, Old Hunstanton and Holme schools. Sonny Middleton was one of the people who helped deliver the meals in steam containers.

The meals service continued until the school closed in the 1980s.

More street scenes

High Street

Left: In 1913 a supporter of the Suffragette Movement held a meeting by the Jubilee Tree. A newspaper report noted:

In spite of the fact that the village is emphatically opposed to the women's suffrage movement, a Miss Brackenbury held a meeting in support thereof the other evening near the Jubilee Tree. After the usual abuse of the Government, questions were invited. An affirmative reply was given to the enquiry, 'Do you think breaking windows and doing wilful damage assists your cause?' 'The public know we are in earnest,' said the speaker.

Below: Green Lane looking towards Herga Cottage before the council houses were built.

GREEN LANE, THORNHAM.

Church Street Thornham.

THE CHAPELS, THORNHAM.

Left, top: View of Church Street and the gates to the Manor.

Bottom: A rare picture of the two Methodist chapels, Wesleyan and Primitive. The latter was demolished in the 1940s. The five cottages behind were demolished in the 1930/40s.

Above: High Street in the 1930s, a time when the Parish Council was already regularly discussing traffic problems. A 1930 minute talks about how the elderly were trying to avoid the High Street at times ... *We have very old men, one of whom is blind, and owing to present-day traffic conditions on the main road, they take their exercise down Staithe Lane ...*

In 1953 increasing summer traffic was causing problems at the Church Street/Main Road junction and the Parish Council called for a speed limit.

Air traffic was also a worry. In 1955 a parishioner asked if the RAF could tell its pilots to fire their rockets/shells into the Thornham beach range in single shots rather than salvoes to cause less noise. That range finally closed a few years later.

THORNHAM. NORFOLK.

Left: A view from the church tower and (below), the King's Head from the air.

Two views of Thornham from the air. The wooded parkland (below) surrounds the Hall. That looks like the old cricket square (bottom right).

The Green

4377. The Green, Thornham

Left: The Green, looking east across the pond, known mysteriously as the *Queen of Sheba*.

THE GREEN, THORNHAM. J 7729. (*Moorhouse's Series.*)

The message on the back of this postcard says that the senders are staying in the Coastguard Cottages, but that they soon move into a property even closer to the sea (almost certainly the Granary which was used pre-war for holidaymakers). The card also says that the 'lookout station' is the cottage on the left, with the 'Coastguard watch room' behind the bottom left-hand window of the right hand cottage. The 'telephone communication' was housed in the gable section of the same house.

Right: The original Oldfield Farm (right) at the eastern end of The Green.

The caption to this 1911 photograph says: 'Hughes Hovel'. In times of hardship and homelessness, people did build their own 'hovel' homes. Perhaps Hughes was a man down on his luck.

The Commiffioners will attend at the Houfe of Jeremiah Johnson, being the sign of the King's Head in Thornham, on Monday the firft Day of December 1794 at eleven o'clock in the Forenoon to receive, hear and determine objections to any such claims…

The purpose of the Commissioners' visit was to settle final agreements with villagers regarding the enclosure of traditional parish lands, designate new roads, paths, rights of way, a common to be used for the collection of firewood, six pits for obtaining building materials, a marsh with rights to collect samphire, dead seagulls and other odds and ends … and 49 common grazing rights on the Green.

Each grazing right allowed the holder to graze:

two cows or heifers, or one cow or one heifer, and one gelding, colt, mare, filly or female ass with or without foal under six months … and we do further order and appoint that no other kind of beast or cattle (except a bull, as hereinafter mentioned) nor any stoned horse … or any infected beast or cattle, nor any geese shall at any time be kept, fed or pastured …. upon the said common …

So whoever was grazing sheep on the common in the picture (previous page) was clearly breaking the rules.

Over the last two centuries those 49 grazing rights became a cash crop in their own right. Many rights were sold or swapped. One rights owner originally bought his from a local doctor, who had, in turn, been given it as payment for medical services.

The current situation is that the Bett family has 46 of the original 49 rights. Miss Margaret Bunkle owns one and the Parish Council was bequeathed the other two by late parishioners Sonny Middleton and Oswald Waterfield. The latter left his to the Council on the condition that it would never be sold.

The Green and rights of way have always been high on the Parish Council agenda. In 1951 there were raised voices over a government initiative to schedule all public footpaths. David Jamieson claimed that one of the supposed paths was a 'd…..! nuisance' as it went through his kitchen garden.

The holders of the original 49 grazing rights as listed in the 1797 Thornham Enclosure Act.

Footnote: Second World War air raid warden Lennie Plume, a former blacksmith and wheelwright and father of Rene Hunt, and Mr Rooke, the Customs Officer, were out on patrol around the Green, when, in the darkness, they spotted a mysterious article lying on the road. The army was immediately alerted and they carefully covered the item for closer inspection in the morning and warned everyone to keep clear. The next day the deadly article was revealed … it was a bread board which Matthew Middleton's dog, notorious for thieving, had stolen from Mrs. Callaby's yard.

Rene also recalls her fear as a teenager when a German bomber swooped low over the Green right above her family home. 'I looked up and I could see the man in the plane and the black swastika on the side. I thought: 'Oh God, he's going to shoot.' It was frightening. Then I heard him fire. I learned later that he had shot at the Coal Barn and Granary.'

[9]

of the feveral Common-Right Houfes in Thornham aforefaid, (exclufive of the Common-Right Houfes and Tofts which belonged to the faid George Hogg, at the time of paffing the faid Act) And that the fame do belong to the feveral Perfons next hereinafter mentioned, as Owners thereof, that is to fay, George Hogg, Efquire in refpect of a Common-able Houfe purchafed by him fince the paffing the faid Act of Frances Jickling, one Right; William Jickling, one; Richard Perkins, one; Ann the Wife of John Evetts, one; William Rofe, two; Sarah the Wife of the faid William Rofe, two; Clement Bell, fix; John Froft and Catherine his Wife, one; Robert Cofton, two; James Cofton, one; Charles Bunn, one; William Dearns, one; Penelope the Wife of James Banyard, one; Robert Forefhaw, one; Alice Large, three; Edward Clarke, one; John Wales, one; Etheldred the Wife of Thomas Curfon, one; Rice Stocking, one; William Woodrow, one; John Clarke, one; William Clarke, one; Elizabeth Bell, one; John Hall, four; George Jickling, one; John Stead, one; William Jarvis, one; Francis Holmes, one; James Dillingham, one; Amy Haycock, one; Richard Dix, one; Hous Iverfon Bofnefs, one; Michael Pattern, one; and Henry Benton, three.

Sporting Days

" Waifs & Strays" Play cricket at Thornham "
'Having tea'

Above: The 'Waifs and Strays' playing cricket at Thornham in 1923. It's thought that the vicar, the Rev. Nathan Waller first invited boys from the Waifs and Strays Society to play against the village side. The Society cared for Britain's many young poor and homeless.

Cricket in the park.

Above: An early Thornham cricket side with a trophy in The Park, possibly the 1920s. The High Street is behind the trees in the background.

Below: Darts was very popular among the Thornham women. (l-r) Mrs. Johnson, Gwen Watson, Cissy Frohawk, Aggie Potter, who was captain of Thornham Conservative Darts Club, Mrs. Arnold, Mrs. Smith, Beattie Hunt, Katy Thompson, Mrs. V. Helsdon, Mrs. Hayter. In more recent times Tim and Daphne Siddle's son Adrian became a county darts player, and also 'chalked' for the world's best.

A Thornham bowls team. Back row (l-r)): Tom Lake, Billy Johnson, Harry Walker, the Reverend Rushmer, Billy Porter, Lewis Mitchell, Arthur Back; mid row: Billy Tipple, Percy Proudfoot, George Raven, George Lee, Vic Helsdon, Benny Howard; front: Harry Bell, Bob Thompson, Jack Walker, Stephen Hewitt.

Marshall Riseborough also played football for the Linnets in Kings Lynn.

A championship Thornham cricket side. (l-r) back row: Charlie Williamson, unidentified, Charlie Hunt, unidentified, Reg Carter, Donny Woods, Reggie Rayner; front: Philip Anderson, Benny Howard, Eddie Bell, Laddie Frohawk and Harry Bustin.

Eddie Bell (above, with trophy) was landlord of the Chequers Inn before, during and after the Second World War. He was Doris Smith's uncle and a Thornham cricket skipper as well as a county player. Doris's son Chris, a later Thornham cricket skipper, was a powerful all-rounder too,

Left: A rare picture of a pre-Second World War Thornham football side. (l-r), back row George Wilson, landlord of the King's Head, Marshall 'Nitch' Riseborough (father of Shirley Lake), Luan Walker, Charlie Riseborough, Dave Stimpson, Tom Lake, Charlie Hunt and Philip Anderson; front row: unidentified, Billy Walker, Eddie Riseborough, Reg Carter, Charlie Goff, uncle of June (née Goff) Fryett, and Darny Mahoney.

Charlie Goff, a member of an old Thornham family, was killed at St. Valery on June 12, 1940. His name is on the Dunkirk memorial.

A young Luan (Llewellyn) Walker, also in the photograph, started work in the Thornham Bakehouse as a lad but gave it up soon after. The Bakehouse meant Saturday afternoon working and young Luan was keener on playing football, so he went to work for the Bett family at Malthouse Farm. Just after the war, Luan broke a leg during a game and had to give up sport. Luan married Edie Parsley. Their son Colin says: 'To my knowledge there is no Welsh side in the family, so I don't know where the Llewellyn comes from. But I know my mother always spelt his name Luan.'

A Thornham Football XI in the 1950s. (l-r) back row: Eddie Riseborough,
Paul Skillings, Dick Johnson, George Misson, ? McFadyen, Harry Johnson (from Brancaster),
Reg Baker; front: Freddie Frohawk, Ivan Bell, George Raven, Peter Smith, Reg Carter and
Gordon Johnson.

A 1950s cricket side. Back row (l-r): Norman Raven, Russell Harwood, captain Graham Raven,
Noel Sutherland, Freddie Frohawk, Alwin Burrell and Billy Walker; front row: John Potter,
Colin Walker, Brian Sadler, Dennis Pooley, David Dawson and Brian Sutherland.

The 1960s. Back row (l-r): Gordon Lake, Malcolm Emmerson, Bruce Jongman, Jimmy Janz and Cecil Rix; front: John Hipkin, John Potter, Alan Walden, Colin Walker, Leo Dolman and Don Playford.

Right: Don Bradman's message to Thornham's skipper, Robert Hinds (below).

DONALD BRADMAN, A.C.

2 HOLDEN STREET,
KENSINGTON PARK,
SOUTH AUSTRALIA 5068.

GOOD LUCK

to

ROBERT HINDS

and

THORNHAM CRICKET CLUB in 1988.

Don Bradman

Humour usually went side-by-side with Thornham sport. Tim Siddle recalls that Cecil Rix (see photo previous page) was playing at centre forward during Thornham's famous 18 goal destruction of Old Town (Old Hunstanton), yet he was the only member of the team not to score. Tim also hints that perhaps Cecil wasn't beyond scoring an own goal or two in his time.

Cecil pleads guilty to the first charge but says of the second: 'That could be right. But if I did score any own goals, then it must have been because the goalkeeper wasn't there when I passed the ball back!'

Tim Siddle spent some time behind the stumps during his cricketing days, placing himself a good twenty yards behind them to face the Thornham speedsters, Graham Raven and Russell Harwood, and even then one of them managed to put a major dent in Tim's box (aluminium in those days).

Cecil Rix was a good cricketing all-rounder too, like his two sons, fiery batsman and bowler Mark and another big family hitter, Simon. Cecil's son-in-law, Robert Hinds, a former Thornham cricket skipper, has a nice bit of cricketing memorabilia. When he was elected captain, a member of the team with Australian connections wrote to Sir Donald Bradman asking if he would drop Robert an encouraging line.

The 'Don' was kind enough to respond. His note read: *Good luck to Robert Hinds and Thornham Cricket Club in 1988.* It was signed Don Bradman.

The annual visit of a touring side known as *The B.....d Trippers* put plenty of humour into village cricket. They toured here for ten years in the 1970s and 80s. On their first trip, the visitors were known simply as *The Trippers.* But it was on that occasion that local man Derek Batterbee (left), drinking in the public bar of the Chequers Inn, heard some rather posh voices coming from the saloon bar. 'B.....d trippers!' joked Derek. The name stuck. A genuine Aussie speedster put terror into the home side that day. But Mark Rix was in the team the following year and claimed all ten wickets. It took the visitors several years to recover from the shock and actually win a game again ... and the trophy, nicknamed 'The Flushes'.

The next generation of the Rix, Siddle, Johnson, Rumbellow and Lake families take to the football field. Back row: Henry Bett, Timothy Arnold, Clive Johnson, Simon Rix, Mark Floyd, Cecil Rix, Howard Floyd, Mark Rix, Adrian Siddle and an official; front row: Jonathon Kipling, Sam Cook, Paul Rumbellow and Jeremy and Stephen Lake.

● Some of the committee of the Thornham Playing Field Association and helpers on their new field which was officially opened on Sunday.

This newspaper photograph includes some of the key people responsible for Thornham getting a new playing field in 1984. (l-r) Colin Burt, John Lake (on the marker), Antony Needham, Sandra Smith and son Jamie, Mary Rutland, Ruth Wyett, Robert Walker and James Rutland.

Others involved in the behind-the-scenes work in running Thornham's league football and cricket included Cecil and Gillian Rix, Shirley Lake, Ken Smalls, Harry Bird, Hugh Whittome, Chris Smith and Adrian Siddle (cricket groundsman for many years).

Out! But still smiling. Adrian 'Sid' Siddle, a stalwart of Thornham cricket.

Sporting Days

Thornham School's football team. (l-r) back row: Russell Farr, Stacey Batterbee, Simon Rix, Paula Jessup, Matthew Batterbee; front: Charlie Wyett, David Langford, Howard Floyd, Adam Bird and John Whiting.

One of the best modern-day football sides. (l-r) back row, Brian Hipkin, Simon Housden, Tim Burgess, Mark Rix, Cecil Rix, Robert Hinds, Steve Walker;
front row: Simon Rix, Andrew Burt, Adam Bird, Stephen Lake, Ron Williamson, Charlie Needham and John Whiting.

The Old Fellas v Thornham CC was one of the most popular cricketing fixtures in the 80s/90s. The caravan masqueraded as a sports hut for a few years and was later replaced by a proper pavilion.

(l-r) back row: Alwyn Burrell, Geoff Cambridge (landlord of the Chequers Inn), Billy Wyett, Aubrey Sadler, Keith Bird, Denny Pooley, Frank Browning; front row: Rodney 'Rodders' Sutherland, Robin Burrell, Alan Sadler, Noel Sutherland, David Smith, Antony Needham, George Bussey, Cecil Rix and Norman Raven. George Bussey was a classy cricketer. He played for Holme C.C., the RAF and Minor Counties cricket.

Thornham People

William Ducker (top left), Thornham shopkeeper, with members of the Thornham Brotherhood on an excursion with his wagon. The Brotherhood was a local branch of a national 19th/early 20th-century men's association. Among those also believed to be in the photograph are coal merchant Frank Callaby, Amos Sutherland, George Howard, James Rason, Reuben Eagle and Charles and Matthew Middleton.

Thornham Women's Institute on parade. The recognisable names here include (roughly l-r) Adie Tipple, Mrs. Davison, Mrs. Hewitt, Doris Cobb, Doris Burrell, Mrs. Eves, Ethel Bell, Mrs. Stimpson, Mrs. Hickman, Mrs. Cobb senior, Helen Gent, Jessie Bush, Beatrice Nudds and Kate Roper.

Sunday School Party 1951: The names here include Miss Healy, Mrs. Ames, Mrs. Rumbellow, Mrs. Greef, June Fryett, Rita Burt, Shirley Riseborough, Gillian Burt, Mrs. Stimpson, Jennifer Bell, the Rev. Russell, Jeanne Smith, Ethel Bell, David Smith, Marilyn Williams, Nelia Cornell, Kate Roper, Eddie Walker and Pauline Burt.

Back (l-r) Freddie Chapman, Alan Greef, Martin Steward, Charlie Groundsell, Alison Chapman, Denise Pooley, Patricia Harwood; front, Jenny Mallett, Billy Pooley, Robert Howell, Tony Godfrey, Douglas Greef, Christine Mallett, Stephen Greef. Teacher Rose King is at the back.

Sunday School Palm Sunday 1973
Back row, Harry Wyett, Russell Farr, Rosemary Kimber, Robert Kimber, Juliette Stone, Rosemary Talbot, Debbie Rix, Marjorie Talbot, Elaine Hinds, Lyn Raven, Julia Crosthwaite, Richard Middleton; front, ? Hughes, Hannah Middleton, Kathryn Large, Stewart Large, Adrian Siddle, Tracey Sutherland, Mark Rix, Shaun Burrell, Angela Whiting, Julie Playford, John Crosthwaite, Hayley Hinds, Alison Chapman, unidentified, Edward Talbot and Hilda Glover's three grandchildren.

In the autumn of their lives ... Ben Howard (brother to Bill), Tom Frohawk and Albert Walker all spent their working lives on the land. Albert, who was married to Millie (née Groundsell), was at Ling Farm for many years.He and Millie had two children, Luan (Llewellyn) and Vera.

The Frohawks were another big Thornham family. Tom, brother to Willy (Winkles), and Lawrence (Laddie), worked on Dick Heading's farm. Ben Howard also worked for Mr Heading. Neither Ben nor his brother Bill married. For a long time they lived with their sister Iris. The two brothers' home in Church Street in later years was always known as *Bill & Ben's Cottage*.

Below: Tim Siddle (left) enjoys a lads' night out. The other boys are (l-r) John Potter, Eric Green, Robin Burrell, Albert Richardson and George Archer.

Young Olive Hart giving pony rides at a 1960s Drove House fête. That's Susie (rear) and Fiona (daughters of David Jamieson VC) aboard. Brenda Flatt's sister Jill is in the background.

The St. Trinian's class on Jubilee Day 1977 (l-r) Tina Johnson, Joanne Rutland, unidentified, Amanda Lake, Olive Johnson (née Hart), Rodney Sutherland, and Alan Greef .

The ship's bell from the minesweeper HMS Thornham was given to Thornham Church in 1967. The ship's commander was Lt. Commander Richard Bridges.

Among the children: front row, Jane Walpole, Alison Chapman, Andrew Burt, Billy Groundsell, Leslie Howell, Rodney Sutherland, Ian Sutherland and Carolyn Fryett; 2nd row, Diana Edge, Jimmy Groundsell, Derek Walker, Debbie Walker.

Summer in the Park, a photograph possibly taken after a cricket match. There are lots of old Thornham family names represented here including Hunt, Howard, Raven, Frohawk, Walker, Helsdon, Baker, Smith, Rix, Bird, Ames and Jacobs.

A late 1940s gathering in the Drill Hall. Back row (standing): Billy Nudds, Lydia Nudds, Mrs. Bertie Fenton, Mrs. Helsdon, Aggie Potter, Bertie Fenton, Mr. Hewitt, unidentified, Ida Wilson, Mrs. Hewitt, Dolly Bird, Frank Stimpson (above), Hannah Monk (below), Ricky Richmond, Emma and Charlie Whiting; sitting (middle row) Louise Hines, Mr. Mitchell, Mrs. Hinton, Mrs. Mitchell, unidentified, Mrs. Rutland, Jacob Rutland, unidentified, Charlie Sayer, George Bell, Billy Richardson, Tom Lake; front: Mrs. Bell, Frances Sadler, Robert Sadler, Morrell Roper, Mrs. Rason, Mr. Rason and Mrs. Raven.

Reg Needham

The Needham family

In 1869 London gunsmith Henry Needham married Emily Hohl, a former member of the royal households of both Queen Victoria and Alexandra, Princess of Wales. Henry's address, 26 Piccadilly, gives some idea of the exquisitely manufactured firearms he made. Today they are highly sought after items.

When the Needhams' first son, Alexander, was born, Princess Alexandra presented the proud parents with a christening cup. The Princess had been friends since the days when Emily was her dresser.

Eighty years on, the couple's great-grandson, Reg Needham and his family set up home in Thornham. A Harrow man, Reg joined the RAF in London at the start of the Second World War. His wife Ivy, and their first five children, Geoff, John, Jean, Molly and Doreen, left London for the relative safety of Norfolk. Soon after, Reg was in action with the 601 County of London Squadron in North Africa, using his specialist joinery skills to work on Spitfires.

After the war, Reg rejoined his family and, in 1949, with two later additions to the family, Wendy and Antony (born in Hunstanton), the family moved into a house in Thornham, where the last child, Susan, was born.

Reg started a building firm and today signs of his work can be seen all over the village; from the council houses behind Castle Cottages to the conversion into a home of the coach house that belonged to the Cottage.

Two of Reg's sons, carpenter John (left) and general builder Antony, work in the village.

Reg Needham's wife Ivy and son Antony after a deluge.

Doris Cobb

The Cobb family

At the bottom of Church Street there is a house called Hendor. The name is a combination of the first names of Henry and Doris Cobb. Henry, a former carpenter, almost single-handedly built the house for his bride.

Henry was the son of Alfred Cobb, who worked as Victor and Violet Ames' gardener at Marshlands. Alfred planted most of the mature trees seen there today. Henry's grandfather, another Henry, was a saddler and harness maker.

Henry Cobb learned his trade as a carpenter during a five year apprenticeship with Mr. Shanks in Hunstanton. That was in the days when, according to Doris, 'if a gap in a joint was the size of a cigarette paper you'd get a clip around the ear.'

Doris was a Buckinghamshire girl and came to Thornham in the 1930s as 'third housemaid' to the Robarts in Thornham Manor.

She met her husband at a dance in the Drill Hall. It was the same night that the

Jamieson's chauffeur, Francis Mitchell, met his bride Nora, head housemaid at The Manor. 'Below stairs' staff at the various big houses tended to mix with each other.

Henry and Doris spent the war away from the village. Henry was at Weybridge doing carpentry work on Wellington bombers. Back in Thornham, Henry worked on many local projects, including interior church work and the lych-gate.

Henry and Doris Cobb on their wedding day in the summer of 1939.

Thornham People

Annie Sutherland, seen here in 1960, was one of the Sutherlands who can trace their family back several generations in Thornham. Annie was David 'Bubbles' Sutherland's great aunt. David married Dorothy Ward, a member of the Ringstead Nursery family. Dorothy, also known as Nellie, worked at the Lifeboat Inn for many years. The couple had three boys, Alan (Ali), Rodney (Rodders) and Paul (Jimbo).

Margaret Rushmer and her brother, the Rev. Rushmer (vicar 1927-46).

Below: A clay pigeon shoot at one of Thornham Manor garden fêtes when Mr. Robarts was in residence. (l-r) Dick Batterbee, Vic Helsdon (Dairy Farm), Arthur (Ricky) Richmond (mushroom farm), David Sutherland and Vincent Sadler (uncle to Olive Waterfield).

Pleasance Bett in Thornham Church when she visited Pat Thompson's exhibition of village photographs which forms the basis for this book.

One of the best remembered images of Pleasance Bett, sister of the late Henry Bett, is of her speeding around the village on a mobility scooter with two Union Jack flags flying proudly from the handlebars. Pleasance, full of the John Bull spirit, defied officialdom and red tape to create a remarkable one-woman company, *Thornit*, to market a treatment for dog canker.

Pleasance's mother had used an old formula to treat her own dog. Much later, Pleasance got a chemist to copy that formula when her dog developed the condition. It worked so well that, in the 1970s, she began marketing it. Pleasance now has loyal customers right around the world. 'I started the business basically because I was told I couldn't,' she explains. 'They kept saying I had to have a licence and all sorts of other things. But I never did get one. I think the authorities gave up on me in the end.'

Pleasance Bett and Joan Ames, on Thornham beach in the 1920s.

Below: A young Pleasance Bett with her brother Henry and their parents, Margaret (née Archdale) and Stafford Henry Imlach Bett.

Christmas 1984: back row, Duncan Rutland, Sarah Brock, Pippa Cable, Bonnie Pooley, Ben Handley, Mark Floyd and Jamie Smith; mid row, Louise Needham, Kirsty Walker, Barry Wright, Sarah Smith, Naomi Brown, Mathew Sils, Angela Brock, Kate Handley; front, Katie Needham, Michael Chamberlain, Anthony Small, Chris Langford and Mathew Moe.

A 1950s Christmas party in the school. The front seat girls are (l-r) Pamela Crown, Audrey Watson, Jenny Bell, Rita Sadler, Pauline Burt and Marigold Brewster.

A night out in Peterborough courtesy of Perkins Diesel Engines for some lads from the farm, and the boss ... (l-r) Luan Walker, Henry Bett, Bob Bussey (rear), (unidentified), Eric Beck and Marshall Riseborough.

Right: A fête at Thornham Manor. Mrs. Robarts, wearing a hat and coat, is sitting in the centre. Edie Maud Walker is sitting down at extreme left. Millie Walker is behind her. Hilda Groundsell is on the left behind the hedge.

Right: A modern-day Thornham Gardens Open Day fundraiser. (l-r) Marjory Webster, Sue Grout, Peter Goff, Patti Gambling, Antony Needham, Ann Goff, Sheila Milner, Charles Milner, Gill Tuffs (Marie Curie), Jennifer Morris, Monica Clare, David Brooks, Wendy Brooks, Glynis Allen, Janet Needham and Terry Morris.

Three pals. Eric Beck (left) and Neville Nudds, and his dog Penny in 2006. Eric and Neville worked together for more than 40 years on Thornham Farms.

Fifty of Ruth Wyett's friends gathered to mark her 1998 retirement as Practice Nurse at Burnham Market Surgery. She had spent 20 years at the practice which looked after the majority of Thornham's population. Ruth also worked at the 'branch office' surgery behind York Cottage.

Monica Clare with Ben Howard in the 1970s and (right) Ben in the Lifeboat.

Duncan Bolt, seen here at a 1980s Thornham Regatta. He and Tim Siddle are both members of the International Guild of Knot Tyers.

Below: Madge Wilkins, who died in 2005, lived at The Poplars in Thornham and ran the Holme riding stables for many years. Here she is (left) with some riders on Thornham Beach in the 1970s.

The village has a new bus shelter, which was built by local craftsmen, including (l-r) Robert Howell (and Kizzie), designer Frank Bradbeer, Antony Needham and Mark Rix. The plaque lists all those involved.

Carole Howell is assistant in the shop. Patti's daughter Ria helps out.

A new shop ... Patti Gambling and Tania Rowell run the new shop, in a building put up for the village by local man 'Spider' Goddard (left).

Making a splash at a 1980s Thornham regatta are (l-r) Robert Howell, Antony Needham, Robbie Wright and Mark Rix.

Right: One of the last photographs of the staff and children of Thornham School which closed in 1985. The staff here include Ann Whiting, Maureen Sutherland, Jenny Jessop, Doreen Wolverson and Dorothy (Nellie) Sutherland.

Builder Robert Howell, aboard his boat *Sally*, leaves harbour on a fishing trip into The Wash; (inset) Robert Howell and Mark Rix, 2006.

A Thornham Wives' Tale

Right: Carolyn Drewry, Tracey Rix and Sandra Smith

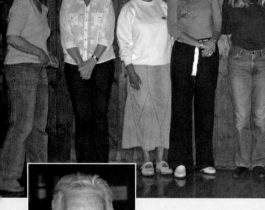

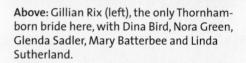

When every house in the village was occupied by local people, marriages between families were usual. Today, with so many second homes, both sexes increasingly look outside the village for partners. Here we salute Thornham wives, born and bred, or from away.

Glenda Sadler (above), who was involved in running the Thornham Young Wives Club, Youth Club and Thornham Guild of Helping Hands (all long gone) now runs a village line dance group. Plenty of Thornham wives in the big line-up above.

Right: Carole Howell, Maggie Pooley and Janet Needham ... three more wives who came to Thornham.

Above: Gillian Rix (left), the only Thornham-born bride here, with Dina Bird, Nora Green, Glenda Sadler, Mary Batterbee and Linda Sutherland.

A Younger Generation – 2006

(l-r) row 1, Matt Batterbee, Sharon & Christopher Langford, Bonnie Pooley & Stacey Batterbee; row 2, Kate & Louise Needham, Adam & Mark Bird; row 3, Tom & Charlie Wyett, Jamie & Sarah Smith, Beverley & Louise Howell; row 4, Emma & Kirsty Rix, Jamie & Robert Sutherland; row 5, Samantha Trett.

Bibliography

The Brancaster Lifeboats – Michael Softley

Norfolk Corn Mills – Harry Apling 1984.

Smugglers All – Kenneth Hipper

A Short History of Thornham – Miss Rushmer 1932

Thornham and Its Story. Miss P.M.A. Bett and F.S. Franklin 1974 and revised edition Charles Milner 2004

Notes on the History of Thornham – Violet Ames

All Saints' Church Thornham – T. Hugh Bryant

Kelly's and *White's* Directories

Thornham Census 1841, 1881 and 1901

The Norfolk Regiment 1685-1918 – F. Loraine Petre

The Royal Norfolk Regiment 1919-1951 – P.K. Kemp

Brancaster Staithe: The Story of a Norfolk Fishing Village – Maurice de Soissons

Account of Wrecks and Disasters which have taken place on the North Norfolk Coast Since 1860 – William Harman

East Anglia 1939 – R. Douglas Brown 1980

The Buildings of England – Pevsner and Wilson

The Origins of Norfolk – Tom Williamson

The Shell Book of Country Crafts – James Arnold

A Dictionary of Old Trades, Titles and Occupations – Colin Waters

Tracing the History of Villages – Trevor Yorke

Norfolk Origins 6: Changing Agriculture in Georgian and Victorian Norfolk – Susanna Wade Martins

Norfolk Origins 8: Exploring the Norfolk Village – Christopher Barringer

The Countryside Remembered – Sadie Wood

The Traditional Farming Year – Paul Heiney

The Turn of the Tide – North Norfolk's Saltmarsh Coast – Edited by Ian Scott

Acknowledgements

This book could not have been produced without the much appreciated help of so many local families and other contributors. They include, in alphabetical order, the following:

Glynis Allen, the late Gwen Baker, the late David Bartram, Derek and Mary Batterbee, Eric Beck, Pleasance, Diana, Stephen and Charles Bett, Harry and Dina Bird, Duncan Bolt, Pamela and Ben Brock, David Brooks, Margaret Bunkle, the Burt family, Bryony Carey and the late Eileen Richmond, Monica Clare, Doris Cobb, Charles Coker, Susan Dearden, Carolyn Drewry, Irene and Raymond Ducker (and Molly Baker of the Ducker family), Les Edgar, Brenda Flatt, Kenny Francis, June Fryett, Patti Gambling, Henry, Desmond and Stephen Greef, Nora Green, Sue Grout, Ellen, Robert and Carole Howell and family, Rene Hunt, Olive Johnson, Peter Jones, John and Shirley Lake, Jenny Langford, Bob Le Masurier, Charles Milner, Marian Montgomery, Janet, Antony, John and Geoff Needham (and Doreen Wilson), Hazel Newman, Neville Nudds, Michael and Jenny Partyka, Maggie Pooley, Charles and Vicky Rangeley-Wilson, the late Ted Rason, Graham Raven, Geoff Renaut, Cecil and Gillian Rix and family, Tania Rowell, Mary Rutland, Glenda Sadler, Tim, Daphne and Adrian Siddle, Richard and Dorothy Sidey, Doris and Sandra Smith and family, Michael Softley, Sam Staveley, Chris Swain, David, Dorothy, Ali and Linda Sutherland, Brenda Sutherland, Rosemary Talbot, Keith Thomson, Peter Tipple, Colin Walker, Marjory Webster, Ann and Tony Whiting and Mark and Ruth Wyett.

In addition we would like to acknowledge the following: Martin Goodsell (for the two maps), the Norwich Millennium Library, the Norfolk Record Office, the Royal Naval Submarine Museum, the Royal Norfolk Regimental Museum, the King's Lynn and Hunstanton libraries, and the Wisbech and Fenland Museum. We also thank Eastern Counties Newspapers, Lynn News and Mirror Newspapers for permission to reprint some of their photographs and for the use of some archive material. Thanks to Jeremy Phipp and Vernon Maldoom for the use of several of the Giles Family Archive photographs.